Mathematical Enrichment Exercises

Exercises

A Teacher's Guide

Dennis Thyer

CASSELL

Cassell
Villiers House
41/47 Strand
London WC2N 5JE, England

387 Park Avenue South
New York, NY 10016–8810
USA

First published 1993

British Library Cataloguing-in-Publication Data
A catalogue record for this book is available from the British Library.

ISBN 0–304–32605–4
    0–304–32591–0 (pbk)

Typeset by Fakenham Photosetting Ltd, Fakenham, Norfolk
Printed and bound in Great Britain by Dotesios Ltd, Trowbridge, Wilts.

Contents

List of Number Activities

List of Shape and Space Activities

List of Puzzlers

Preface

This book contains sets of enrichment exercises, which are mainly investigative, at Levels 2, 3, 4, 5 and 6 of the National Curriculum in Mathematics of England and Wales. Most of the sets include enough questions of the same type to enable pupils to practise the strategies and skills involved.

The activities have been carefully selected for junior and lower secondary school pupils and require the use of mathematical ideas and skills within a variety of contexts. More than 400 questions are included involving number, money, measures, shape and space, and logical thinking, from which the teacher may select appropriate exercises for inclusion into individual learning programmes. Worked examples and solution hints, which may prove helpful to the teacher, are also given.

The content should prove valuable for junior school teachers, mathematics teachers of pupils in their middle years, and trainee teachers pursuing courses directed at these stages in departments or faculties of education in colleges and universities, when preparing mathematical work for children.

The activities provide opportunities to apply mathematics in interesting, and often recreational, situations. The idea that mathematics can be pleasurable and captivating is not often appreciated, yet questions of the kind included in this text help to develop creative potential and intellectual power and may also provide enjoyment.

Using This Book

The activities in this text have been arranged in three categories: Number, Shape and Space, and Puzzlers. Some of these demand mainly arithmetical skills whilst others require predominantly spatial ideas. Those questions included in Puzzlers concern more the finding of hidden relationships or numbers, and require logical thought, yet all mathematics demands this to a greater or lesser extent. Most of the questions are investigative in nature and require various searches along carefully selected paths in order to obtain solutions.

Each category contains sets of questions of a similar nature, or concern a similar theme, often at different levels, and an attempt has been made to arrange activities in order of increasing difficulty. The teacher needs to browse through the exercises and select those at appropriate knowledge and skill levels for the pupils concerned.

The sets of questions in the Number section have been arranged with those involving numbers less than a hundred coming first, followed by those requiring numbers up to a thousand, and finally those needing thousands or more. No particular significance, however, should be attached to the order of presentation of the exercises in Shape and Space, and Puzzlers.

The included activities are mainly at Levels 2, 3, 4 and 5, with a few at Level 6, of the National Curriculum in Mathematics. The questions in most of the sets are not intended to be done one after the other over a period of a few days, or weeks, because they often require different attainment levels. Teachers may initially select Level 2 activities from various sets and, when appropriate, Level 3 questions, and later still, those at Levels 4, 5 and 6. These enrichment exercises need dovetailing into children's individual learning programmes in order that mathematical ideas and skills may be practised and applied as part of their development.

Many books do not contain enough questions for children to practise with and so to learn and master the routines and techniques required. With each new type of question the child will probably need assistance from the teacher which may then be followed by practice exercises in order to learn the procedures involved. This text tries to cater for this need.

Teachers are advised to work through *all* questions *before* setting them to the children. This is necessary in order to appreciate the thought processes and mathematical ideas involved, and to be aware of any calculation which may be needed. One is then in a strong position to select an appropriate question for a child and this is a necessary condition for success.

In addition, the teacher who has worked through a problem beforehand will be able to help pupils do that question because the experiences gained form a basis for discussion. He or she will be aware of the steps to follow in order to obtain the solution and may have found more than one way of reaching it. One particular method may be better for children to use, should help be requested, because it is easier to explain and understand or involves less mathematical knowledge. Some questions may be subdivided into two or more parts which when successfully answered will contribute to a full solution.

Pupils, left to themselves for too long, often 'finish' an exercise, but only obtain one, or a few, of the answers in the full solution. This is caused by not having a strategy which embraces all possible events or requirements. The teacher needs to talk with those pupils and guide them along more systematic and orderly paths.

Often the recording of intermediate steps, in a specialized way, can help to clarify a child's thinking. A piece of apparatus, a model, the drawing of a diagram or the use of specially prepared recording sheets can often prove invaluable. Being fully acquainted with the question enables discussion to take place between teacher and pupil which may focus the child's thinking, and the subsequent procedures, along profitable channels.

Most of the sections include comments for the teacher about the questions proposed. These comments vary in content and may contain solution hints, worked examples, details about recording and any special apparatus or grid paper which may be required. Many of the solution hints, and worked examples, suggest methods and procedures which have been successfully used by students and teachers in local schools with junior and lower secondary classes.

The use of calculators needs to be encouraged because they eliminate possible drudgery from repetitive or difficult arithmetic, lead to speedier solutions, and so help to maintain interest.

Some questions contain people's first names and surnames. These may be changed by the teacher where necessary, and other more appropriate or familiar names substituted.

Solutions to the exercises are included at the back of this book.

Number Activities

N1 *Sharing Lemonade and Bottles*

(ANSWERS PAGE 141)

FOR SOLUTION

1. Without pouring lemonade from one bottle to another, share 5 full bottles of lemonade, 5 half-bottles of lemonade and 5 empty lemonade bottles equally among three children so that each one receives the same amount of lemonade and the same number of bottles.

2. Without pouring lemonade from one bottle to another, share 7 full bottles of lemonade, 7 half-bottles of lemonade and 7 empty lemonade bottles among three children so that each one receives the same amount of lemonade and the same number of bottles.

3. Share, without any pouring, 8 full bottles of lemonade, 8 half-bottles and 8 empty bottles, among (a) 3 children, and then (b) 6 children, so that each one receives the same amount of lemonade and the same number of bottles.

COMMENTS

A pencil, a piece of paper, and the abbreviations F (full bottle), H (half-bottle) and E (empty bottle) will help the working out of these questions. The task is to put the appropriate number of these letters into the required number of sets so that the amount of liquid in each is the same, as well as the number of bottles. Questions 2 and 3 have more than one solution. The writing down of letters will help this sharing and the recording of what is being done and what has already been discovered.

N2 *Finding Possible, and Particular, Scores on Special Dartboards*

(ANSWERS PAGE 141)

FOR INVESTIGATION

1. Three darts are thrown at a board (Fig. 1.1) and all score. What possible totals could be obtained? Which is least? Which is greatest? What scores are easiest to obtain? Which are hardest to obtain?

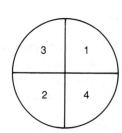

Fig. 1.1

2. Suppose three darts are thrown at a board (Fig. 1.2) and each scores. What possible totals could be obtained? Which is greatest? Which is least? What are the different ways of scoring 10?

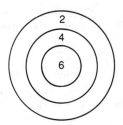

Fig. 1.2

3. Three darts are thrown at a board (Fig. 1.3) and all make a score. What possible totals could be obtained? How could a total of 9 be obtained? Can a score of 10 be obtained in more ways than a score of 11?

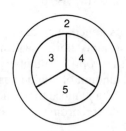

Fig. 1.3

4. Four darts are thrown at a board (Fig. 1.4) and all score, the total score being 20. What may these four scores be if:

   (a) all darts score a different number;
   (b) only two of the darts score the same; and
   (c) three of the darts score the same?

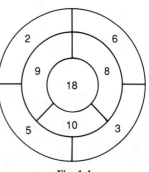

Fig. 1.4

5. Three darts are thrown at a board (Fig. 1.5) and all score. How many different ways are there of obtaining a total of 45? (Note – getting 5, then 15, then 25 is considered to be the same as getting 15, then 5, then 25.)

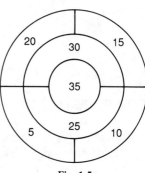

Fig. 1.5

COMMENTS

Possible scores may be investigated by considering what happens should all darts score differently, then two darts score the same, and three darts score the same.

N3 *Obtaining Particular Scores on a Normal Dartboard*

(ANSWERS PAGE 142)

FOR INVESTIGATION

1. Find 8 ways of scoring a total of 50, on a normal dartboard, if all three darts score a different single number.

2. Find 8 ways of scoring a total of 52, on a normal dartboard, if all three darts score, one scoring a double and the other two darts different single numbers.

3. Find 8 ways of scoring exactly 67 on a normal dartboard if three darts are thrown and one scores a treble, one a double and the other a single.

COMMENTS

Pupils need to be familiar with a normal dartboard, and various ways of obtaining scores, for these questions. The following suggestions may also prove helpful.

Question 1

Choose a number, then split the remainder into two unequal numbers.

Question 2

Select a double, then divide the remainder into two unequal numbers.

Question 3

Select the treble, then a double from the remainder. The number left will be the third score. Make these selections smaller if this procedure cannot be carried out.

N4 *Finding Possible, and Particular, Scores at a Shooting Gallery*

(ANSWERS PAGE 142)

FOR INVESTIGATION

1. Discs in a shooting gallery are arranged as shown in Fig. 1.6. When a disc is hit it falls backwards and cannot be hit again. Find, with three scoring shots:

   (a) the least and greatest possible scores;
   (b) different ways of scoring a total of 32;
   (c) ways of scoring a total of 16 or less; and
   (d) ways of scoring a total of 38 or more.

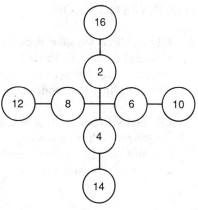

Fig. 1.6

2. Discs in a shooting gallery, arranged as shown in Fig. 1.7, fall backwards when hit and cannot be hit again. How many different ways are there of scoring a total of 15 or more if three shots are fired which all score?

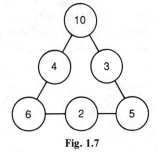

Fig. 1.7

COMMENTS

Find those shots which provide the greatest and least scores. This information should prove helpful when selecting shots to meet other scores.

N5 *Length*

(ANSWERS PAGES 142–3)

FOR INVESTIGATION

1. Obtain three wooden rods 6 cm, 8 cm and 9 cm in length from a Cuisenaire or Colour Factor set. Show how these rods could be used, singly or together, to measure out distances of 6 cm, 14 cm, 15 cm, 17 cm, 2 cm and 3 cm. What other distances, in whole centimetres, may be marked out?

2. Obtain five wooden rods of length 3, 5, 6, 8 and 10 cm from a Cuisenaire or Colour Factor set. What distances, longer than 10 cm, could be measured out using two or more rods placed only end to end? What distances between 10 cm and 32 cm could not be measured out?

COMMENTS

Other distances may be obtained by putting two or more rods end to end, or by putting them side by side in rows with one end of each row being coincident. Apply addition, subtraction, or both.

N6 *Colouring Badges, Mainly*

(ANSWERS PAGE 143)

FOR INVESTIGATION

1. The badge shown in Fig. 1.8 is to be coloured red, green and blue. How many different badges could be coloured in?

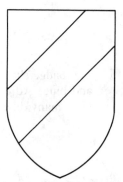

Fig. 1.8

2. The badge shown in Fig. 1.9 is to be coloured red, yellow and blue. Adjoining regions must be of different colours. How many different possible badges could be coloured in?

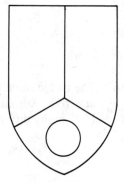

Fig. 1.9

3. Christmas crackers are made from a piece of coloured paper with a paper band surrounding its middle, as shown in Fig. 1.10. Each cracker has a band different in colour to that of its body. Coloured paper and bands are available in red, green, blue and yellow. How many different colour possibilities are there for making crackers?

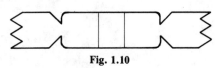

Fig. 1.10

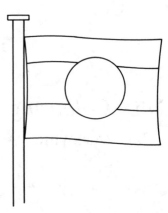

4. How many different ways of colouring the flag red, white and blue are there if adjoining regions must be of different colours? See Fig. 1.11.

Fig. 1.11

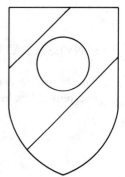

5. The badge shown in Fig. 1.12 is to be coloured red, green and blue. Adjoining regions must have different colours. How many different badges can be formed?

Fig. 1.12

6. The badge shown in Fig. 1.13 is to be coloured yellow, blue and red. Adjoining regions must have different colours. How many different badges could be coloured in?

Fig. 1.13

7. Badges are to be made to the design indicated in Fig. 1.14 and coloured in a symmetrical way. How many different possible badges are there if red, green, blue and yellow are available, each section being only one of these colours, and no adjacent sections the same colour?

Fig. 1.14

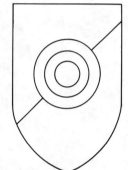

8. The badge shown in Fig. 1.15 is to be coloured red, green and blue. How many different possible badges are there if adjoining regions must have different colours?

Fig. 1.15

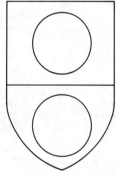

9. The badge in Fig. 1.16 is to be coloured yellow, white and black. How many different colour arrangements are there for possible badges if adjoining regions must have different colours?

Fig. 1.16

COMMENTS

A useful strategy is to assign a colour to a selected region and then investigate, and colour in, various colour choices for the remaining regions. Following this, assign each of the other colours to the initially chosen region, in turn. This procedure enables a prediction to be made about the total number of possible badges, or flags, without necessarily colouring them all in. For example, should 6 possible badges be coloured in when a central stripe is red we would know that a colour change for this stripe would produce 6 more badges. For three different colours of stripe, therefore, the number of possible badges is $6 + 6 + 6$, or 18. A suitable region to select on a badge, as a starting place, is often a centrally positioned circle, stripe or other shape.

A specially prepared recording sheet, which shows the badge, cracker or flag drawn a sufficient number of times, is needed with each question, if the number to be coloured in is reasonably small.

N7 *Colour Selections*

(ANSWERS PAGE 143)

FOR INVESTIGATION

1. There is a large supply of red, blue and green straws of the same length. How many different colours of triangle could be made if any 3 straws are selected and put together, end to end?

2. A large supply of red, green, yellow and blue straws is available of the same length. How many different colours of triangle could be made if any 3 straws are selected and put together, end to end?

3. There is a large supply of blue, green and yellow straws of the same length. How many differently coloured squares could be formed if any 4 straws are selected and put together, end to end?

4. A necklace is made with 5 beads, some yellow and some red. Investigate, and draw, different possible bead arrangements for these necklaces made with 1 yellow and 4 red beads, 2 yellow and 3 red beads, and so on. How many different 5-bead necklaces are possible?
    Repeat this activity using 6 beads, some red and some yellow.

5. In the rectangle shown in Fig. 1.17 each of the sections may be coloured red, blue or green. How many different ways can the rectangle be coloured if all three colours are used?

    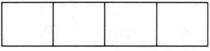
    Fig. 1.17

    (Colour in, on squared paper, different arrangements for 2 red, 1 blue and 1 green section. Then use the result to *predict* the total number of different ways when other colour choices are made.)

COMMENTS

The following suggestions may be useful.

Question 1

Select 3 straws of the same colour, then 2 straws the same colour, then all straws different colours.

Question 3

Select 4 straws the same colour, then 3 straws the same colour, then 2 straws the same colour.

Question 4

Make necklaces with 1 red bead and 5 yellow beads, 2 red and 4 yellow beads, and so on. Make sure there are no repeats should the necklaces be turned over or rotated.

N8 *Dominoes*

(ANSWERS PAGES 143–4)

Each of the following activities requires the use of the 28 dominoes from a double-six domino set.

1. Select 2 dominoes which have a total of 4 dots. How many different possible ways are there of doing this? Sketch them.

2. Select 2 dominoes which have a total of 5 dots. How many different possible ways are there of doing this? Sketch them.

3. Select 3 dominoes which have a total of 5 dots. How many different sets of 3 dominoes can you find with this property? Sketch them.

4. Find sets of 3 different dominoes which may be arranged to form additions which make 52. The dots on the dominoes, read left to right, represent tens and units digits as shown in Fig. 1.18.

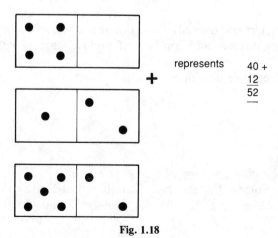

Fig. 1.18

In this case also treat $12 + 40$ and $40 + 12$ as being the same addition. Can you find 10 different ways?

5. Find sets of 3 different dominoes which may be arranged to form subtractions with answers of 42. The dots on the dominoes, read from left to right, represent tens and units digits as shown in Fig. 1.19.

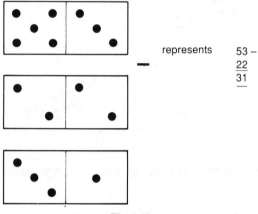

represents

$$\begin{array}{r} 53 - \\ 22 \\ \hline 31 \\ \hline \end{array}$$

Fig. 1.19

Can you find 14 different subtractions?

COMMENTS

Pupils should be familiar with the normal 28 piece double-six domino set. Domino arrangements, or selections, arising from these questions may be recorded by drawing them on squared paper.

Questions 1–3

The child needs to select and use only those dominoes whose individual dot totals are 5 or less. The writing down of addition facts of 4 and 5 suggests paths to follow, e.g.
4: $4 + 0$, $3 + 1$ and $2 + 2$ 5: $5 + 0$, $4 + 1$ and $3 + 2$
   Translate these facts into dominoes.

Question 4

The statement that
$52 = 52 + 0 = 51 + 1 = 50 + 2 = \ldots = 28 + 24 = 27 + 25$
could be applied. Some of these facts can be illustrated with dominoes, e.g.
$51 + 1 = 52$; others cannot, e.g. $52 + 0 = 52$, $48 + 4 = 52$ and $43 + 9 = 52$.

Question 5

The statement that
$42 = 42 - 0 = 43 - 1 = 44 - 2 = \ldots = 65 - 23 = 66 - 24$
could be applied. Some of these facts can be illustrated with dominoes, e.g.
$43 - 1 = 42$; others cannot, e.g. $42 - 0 = 42$, $48 - 6 = 42$ and $51 - 9 = 42$.

N9 *Unequal Partitioning of Sets*

(ANSWERS PAGE 144)

FOR SOLUTION

1. I have 65 beads, some red and some blue. There are 7 more red beads than blue ones. How many beads are there of each colour?

2. There are 58 beads coloured red, white or yellow. There are 4 more red beads than white beads, and 3 more white beads than yellow beads. How many beads are there of each colour?

3. I have 36 buttons in 4 different colours. There are twice as many white buttons as green ones. There are 7 more red buttons than green buttons, and 1 more green button than blue buttons. How many buttons are there of each colour?

4. There are 40 cubes in 4 different colours. There are 5 fewer red cubes than green cubes, 10 more red cubes than white cubes, and 8 more green cubes than blue cubes. How many cubes are there of each colour?

COMMENTS

Example

There are 65 beads coloured white, red or yellow. There are 6 more red beads than yellow beads and 8 more white beads than red beads. How many beads are there of each colour?

This question could be done using a trial and improvement method as illustrated in Fig. 1.20.

white	red	yellow	total	
18	10	4	32	too small
28	20	14	62	too small
30	22	16	68	too large
29	21	15	65	just right

Fig. 1.20

There are 29 white, 21 red and 15 yellow beads.

This kind of approach may be used to answer the questions in this section.

N10   *How Many and How Old?*

(ANSWERS PAGE 144)

FOR SOLUTION

1. A woman has 4 children. The eldest is 3 years older than the second child, who is 3 years older than the third child, who is 3 years older than the youngest child. The youngest child is one half the age of the oldest child. How old are the children?

2. I had some sweets. I ate half of them and then gave 3 sweets to Debbie. I ate half the remainder and then gave another 3 sweets to Debbie. No sweets were then left. How many sweets did I have at the start?

3. Sabree had some sweets. She ate half the sweets and half a sweet, then gave Jade half the sweets left and half a sweet, then gave Gary half the sweets left and half a sweet. She then had no sweets left. How many sweets did she have at the start?

4. Kylie, Zamund and Jane collect foreign coins. Kylie and Zamund altogether have 28 coins. Zamund and Jane together have 32 coins. Kylie and Jane altogether have 40 coins. How many coins do the 3 children have altogether, and how many does each one have?

COMMENTS

Example

Adam had some sweets. He ate half of them and gave 2 sweets to Pippa. He then ate half the remainder and gave 2 more sweets to Pippa. No sweets were then left. How many sweets did he have at the start?

This question may be done by trial and improvement as shown in Fig. 1.21.

start	ate	gave to Pippa	sweets left	ate	gave to Pippa	sweets left	
20	10	2	8	4	2	2	too many at start
16	8	2	6	3	2	1	too many at start
14	7	2	5	2½	*	*	halves not allowed
12	6	2	4	2	2	0	just right

Fig. 1.21

Adam had 12 sweets at the start.

The questions in this section may be done using this approach but each will need its own particular layout for recording the results.

N11 *Inserting Missing Numbers in Diagrams to Fulfil Particular Requirements*

(ANSWERS PAGES 144–6)

FOR INVESTIGATION

1. Put only the numbers 2, 3 and 4 on the grid shown in Fig. 1.22, one number in each square, so that the 3 numbers in each row, each column and each diagonal have the same total.

Fig. 1.22

2. Arrange the numbers from 1 to 7, inclusive, one number in each circle of Fig. 1.23, such that the 3 numbers in each row have the same total. How many different ways can you find?

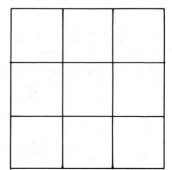

Fig. 1.23

3. Arrange the numbers from 1 to 9, inclusive, one number in each circle of Fig. 1.24, so that the 3 numbers in each of the 4 rows have the same total as the others. How many different ways can you find to do this?

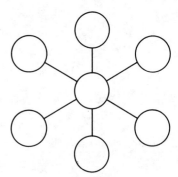

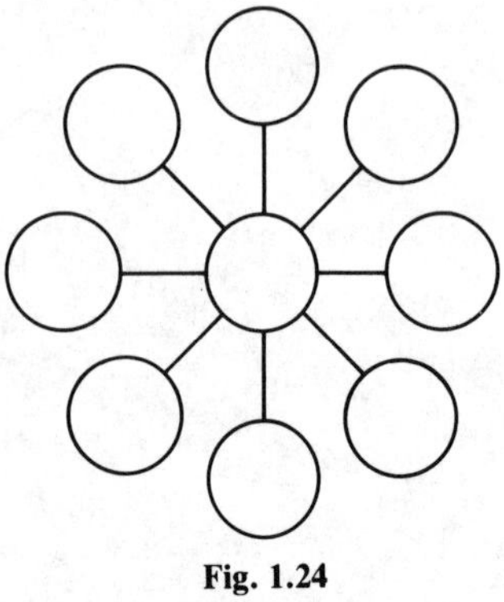

Fig. 1.24

4. Put all the numbers 1, 2, 3, 5, 7, 9 and 10 on the diagram shown in Fig. 1.23, one number in each circle, so that the 3 numbers in each of the 3 rows have the same total.

5. Put the numbers 3, 5, 6, 8 and 9 on the grid shown in Fig. 1.25, one number per square, so that the sum of the 3 numbers in the row (across) equals the sum of the 3 numbers in the column (up and down).

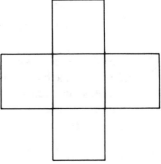

Fig. 1.25

6. Choose different numbers from 1, 2, 3, 4, 5 and 6. Put any 5 of these, one number per square, on the grid shown in Fig. 1.25, such that the 3 numbers in the row across add to the same total as the 3 numbers in the column, up and down.

7. Choose any 5 of the numbers 0, 1, 2, 3, 4, 5, 6, 7, 8 and 9, and put them on the grid shown in Fig. 1.25, one number per square, so that the sum of the 4 outer numbers equals the inner central number.

8. Choose 5 numbers from 1, 2, 3, 4, 5, 6 and 7. Put them, one number per square, onto the grid shown in Fig. 1.25, such that the sum of the 4 outer numbers equals twice the central number.

9. Choose 5 different numbers from 1, 2, 3, 4, 5, 6 and 7, and put them, one number per square, on the grid shown in Fig. 1.25, such that the sum of the 4 outer numbers is three times the inner central number.

10. The numbers 1, 2 and 3 are placed at the corners of a triangle as shown in Fig. 1.26. Arrange the numbers 4, 5, 6, 7, 8 and 9 on the sides of the triangle, one number in each circle, such that the numbers on each side add to 17.

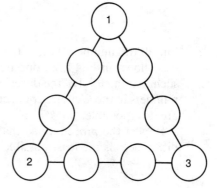

Fig. 1.26

11. Using Fig. 1.26, the numbers 7, 8 and 9 are placed at the corners of the triangle. Put the numbers 1, 2, 3, 4, 5 and 6 along the sides so that the 4 numbers on each side add to 23.

12. Again using Fig. 1.26, the numbers 5, 8 and 10 are placed at the corners of the triangle. Arrange the numbers 1, 2, 3, 4, 6 and 7 on the sides, one number in each circle, so that the numbers on each side add to 23. Can you find 2 different ways of doing this?

13. Use all the numbers 1, 2, 3, 4, 5 and 6. Put one number in each circle of Fig. 1.27 such that the 3 numbers on each side of the triangle have the same total.

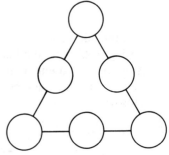

Fig. 1.27

14. Put the numbers 1, 2, 3, 4 and 6 in the circles shown in Fig. 1.28, one number per circle, such that the total of all the differences between the numbers in those circles connected by lines is the greatest possible.

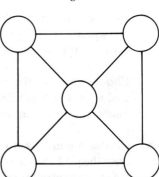

Fig. 1.28

15. Put all the numbers 1, 2, 3, 4, 5 and 6 in the circles shown in Fig. 1.29, one number per circle, such that the total of the differences between the numbers in those circles connected by lines is the greatest possible.

Repeat the procedure so that the total of the differences is the least possible.

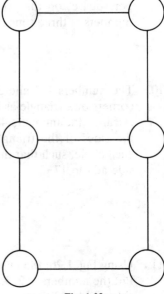

Fig. 1.29

COMMENTS

Special recording sheets need to be prepared for many of the questions in this section. Ensure that these sheets contain more than enough diagrams to cater for possible answers.

Questions 2–4

Put each of the given numbers in the central circle, in turn, and arrange all the remaining numbers in pairs, each pair having the same total. To reduce the number of solutions, take into account *only* different central numbers. Different possible placings of the rows of three numbers may be ignored, each being considered to produce the same solution.

Questions 5–9

Consider putting each of the given numbers into the central square, in turn, and then examine the remaining numbers and allocate some of them according to the requirements demanded. Answers may be worked out and recorded on centimetre squared paper.

Questions 5 and 6 are easier to manage if the numbers of possible answers are reduced. This may be done by considering those solutions which are reflections or rotations of each other, such as those illustrated below, to be the same.

```
      1            1            5            3
  5   2   3    3   2   5    1   2   4    4   2   1
      4            4            3            5
```

Different placings of the four outer numbers, in questions 7–9, may also be considered to be the same solution; see below.

```
      3            3            4            3
  4   9   1    1   9   7    7   9   1    4   9   7
      7            4            3            1
```

Questions 10–12

Find the totals of the missing pairs of numbers on each side of the triangle. Examine the available numbers and pair them to gain these totals. Different placings of the missing numbers along the sides may all be considered to produce the same answer, as shown below.

```
        0                0                0
      8   6            4   5            4   6
    4       5        8       6        8       5
  1   7   3   2    1   7   3   2    1   3   7   2
```

Question 13

Put into the corner circles, in turn, odd numbers, even numbers, two odd and one even number, two even and one odd number. Explore these possibilities.

N12 *How Many? Numbers of Things from Two or Three Categories*

(ANSWERS PAGES 146–7)

COMMENTS

The problems in this category need systematic approaches otherwise solutions may be missed. The following examples illustrate methods of approach and recording procedures which prove helpful for children to use.

Example 1

I see horses and people. Altogether there are 10 heads and 26 legs. How many are there of each?

If there are 10 heads we know there are 9 horses and 1 person, or 8 horses and 2 people, and so on. Test some of these possibilities, recording the results as shown in Fig. 1.30.

no. of horses	no. of horses' legs	no. of people	no. of people's legs	Total no. of legs
9	36	1	2	38
7	28	3	6	34
5	20	5	10	30
3	12	7	14	26

Fig. 1.30

There are 3 horses and 7 people.

Example 2

Lollies cost 4p each and chewies cost 3p each. Jennie buys some of each and spends 26p altogether. What may she have bought?

Since 6 lollies cost 24p and 7 lollies cost 28p, she could not buy more than 6 lollies. Consider buying 1, 2, 3, 4, 5 and 6 lollies, in turn, and see whether chewies can be bought with the remaining money, that is, whether the remaining money is a multiple of 3p. These calculations may be recorded as shown in Fig. 1.31. A calculator may be used, if necessary.

no. of lollies	cost of lollies	amount of money left	no. of chewies
1	4p	22p	x
2	8p	18p	6
3	12p	14p	x
4	16p	10p	x
5	20p	6p	2
6	24p	2p	x

Fig. 1.31

Jennie may have bought 5 lollies and 2 chewies, or 2 lollies and 6 chewies.

Example 3

Apples cost 8p, oranges 10p and pears 6p each. Francis bought some of each and spent 62p altogether. What may he have bought?

Select the dearest item and buy 1, 2, 3, ..., in turn, and explore the buying of the other two items with the remaining money. The working out and recording could be similar to that shown in Fig. 1.32.

oranges bought	amount left	no. of apples	cost of apples	money remaining	no. of pears
1	52p	1	8p	44p	x
		2	16p	36p	6
		3	24p	28p	x
		4	32p	20p	x
		5	40p	12p	2
		6	48p	4p	x
2	42p	1	8p	34p	x
		2	16p	26p	x
		3	24p	18p	3
		4	32p	10p	x
		5	40p	2p	x
3	32p	1	8p	24p	4
		2	16p	16p	x
		3	24p	8p	x
4	22p	1	8p	14p	x
		2	16p	6p	1
5	12p	1	8p	4p	x

Fig. 1.32

So Francis may have bought

oranges	apples	pears
1	2	6
1	5	2
2	3	3
3	1	4
4	2	1

FOR SOLUTION

1. Ben keeps guinea-pigs and his father keeps pigeons. Altogether their animals have 10 heads and 34 legs. How many guinea-pigs did Ben have?

2. A pen in the community farm contained only rabbits and chickens. Altogether these animals had 17 heads and 42 legs. How many animals were there of each kind?

3. In the park, Mohammed saw people and dogs. Altogether he counted 22 heads and 68 feet. Were there more dogs than people?

4. A hunter returned with 25 heads and 80 feet. If he only brought back rabbits and pigeons, how many did he have of each kind?

5. In the park, Hannah counted 16 wheels altogether on bicycles and tricycles. How many bicycles and tricycles may she have seen?

6. A furniture shop had on display some 3-legged stools and 4-legged chairs. Altogether there were 29 legs on this furniture. How many chairs and stools may have been on display?

7. Ann collected some beetles and spiders. Altogether they had 54 legs. What may she have collected?

8. There are 6-wheeler and 4-wheeler lorries in a haulage depot. Altogether there were 56 wheels touching the ground. How many 6-wheelers and 4-wheelers may there have been?

9. Chokkies cost 4p and Fruities cost 5p. Altogether some of each were bought and 90p spent. How many of each may have been bought?

10. Dennis, John and Rachel each spend 48p and buy both chocolate and fruit sweets. Chocolate sweets cost 3p and fruit sweets cost 4p. Dennis buys twice as many fruit sweets as John, and twice as many chocolate sweets as Rachel. What did each of the children buy?

11. The 'shapes' box contains triangles, rectangles, pentagons and hexagons. Elizabeth picked out 3 shapes, not necessarily all different, and found that they had 12 sides altogether. What may she have picked out?

12. Minties cost 3p, Toffos cost 5p and Fruitos cost 7p. Altogether I spend 30p and buy some of all these kinds of sweets. What may I have bought? Which solution provides most packets of sweets?

13. Fizzos cost 2p each, Fruities cost 4p each and Chewies cost 6p each. Mary bought some of each and spends 20p altogether. What may she have purchased?

14. The Speedies were doing their circus act using tricycles, bicycles and unicycles. Altogether there were 9 wheels in the ring and all three kinds of cycle. If there were more tricycles than bicycles, how many Speedies were there and what were they riding?

15. One pound was spent buying plastic farm animals: a sheep costs 10p, a pig costs 15p and a cow costs 20p. Some of all these kinds were bought. What may have been purchased?
    What is the greatest number, and the least number, of animals which could have been bought?
    If 8 animals were bought, what were they?

16. Tea costs 40p, Coke 45p and coffee 60p. Lucille and her 7 friends went into a cafe and bought some of each. They had only one drink each and the total bill amounted to £4.10. What did they buy?

N13 *Areas of Rectangles*

(ANSWERS PAGE 148)

FOR SOLUTION

1. A rectangle has an area of 48 sq. cm. It is 2 cm longer than it is wide. What size is the rectangle?

2. A rectangular carpet is twice as long as it is wide. Another rectangular carpet is 1 m shorter and 1 m wider than the previous one but its area is 2 sq. m more. What are the sizes of the carpets?

COMMENTS

The pupil needs to understand that
the area of a rectangle = number of squares in a row × number of rows
or an alternative wording. The dimensions may be found using trial and improvement.

Example

A rectangle is 3 cm longer than it is wide and its area is 88 sq. cm. How long is it?

length	width	area	
10	7	70	too small
12	9	108	too large
11	8	88	just right

The rectangle is 11 cm long.

N14 *Money – Ways of Paying Amounts, Mainly*

(ANSWERS PAGES 148–9)

INVESTIGATIONS

1. Indicate how to pay 68p using 5 coins, 6 coins, 7 coins, ..., 17 coins and 18 coins.

2. Make 72 pence using 3 coins, 5 coins, 6 coins, 7 coins, 8 coins and 16 coins.

3. Make £1 with 27 coins.

4. Imran has 5 pockets in his clothes. In each pocket he has only one coin and all these coins are of different values. Altogether he has 78p. Identify the coins he has.

5. Michael said he had one coin in each of his 7 pockets, that all these coins were different, and that altogether he had £1.86. Was he telling the truth?

6. I have at least one of each British coin and less than £2 altogether. How much may I have?

7. All bananas are the same price and all apples another price. If 3 bananas and 2 apples cost 41p, whilst 2 bananas and 2 apples cost 32p, what does an apple cost?

8. You have one 2p, one 5p and one 10p. What amounts could you pay exactly with all, or some, of these coins, if no change is given?
   Suppose instead you have one 1p, one 2p and two 5p coins. What exact amounts could now be paid?

9. Using coins selected from a supply of 1p, 2p, 5p and 10p coins, find how many different ways there are of paying exactly 10p.

10. Using coins selected from a supply of 1p, 2p, 5p and 10p, find how many dif-

ferent ways there are of paying out 2p, 3p, 4p, ..., 9p and 10p. Enter your results in a table as shown in Fig. 1.33, e.g.

4p: 1p + 1p + 1p + 1p *or* 2p + 2p *or* 2p + 1p + 1p
gives 3 ways altogether.

Amount	2p	3p	4p	5p	6p	7p	8p	9p	10p
No. of ways			3						

Fig. 1.33

11. In how many different ways can you make £1 with 90, or more, coins? Record these various ways.

COMMENTS

Some pupils may need to use plastic money in order to gain solutions. A thorough knowledge of British coinage is also necessary.

N15 Putting Numbers into Sets under Prescribed Conditions

(ANSWERS PAGES 149–51)

EXAMPLES

1. Move a number from one of the sets shown in Fig. 1.34 to another to make the sum of the numbers in each set the same.

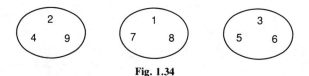

Fig. 1.34

2. Arrange the numbers $1, 4, 5, 6, 7$ and 9 into two sets such that each set has the same sum.

3. Put the numbers $1, 2, 3, 4, 7, 8$ and 9 into two sets, each set of numbers having the same total. How many different ways can you find to do this?

4. Arrange the numbers $1, 3, 5, 7, 9, 11$ and 12 into two sets such that the numbers in each set have the same total.

5. Put the numbers $2, 4, 5, 8, 9$ and 11 into three sets such that each set of numbers has the same sum.

6. Put the numbers $1, 2, 3, 4, 5, 6, 7, 8$ and 9 into three sets such that each set has the same sum. How many different ways can you find to do this?

7. Put all the numbers $1, 2, 3, 4, 5, 6, 7, 8$ and 9, inside or outside a circle, so that the numbers on the outside add to twice the total of the numbers on the inside. Each number must only be used once. Find different possible answers if, inside the circle, there are only (a) two numbers, (b) three numbers, and (c) four numbers.

8. Put the numbers $3, 5, 13, 15, 18, 21$ and 25 into two sets so that the difference between the sums of the numbers in each of the sets is the least possible.

9. Put the numbers $5, 9, 15, 22, 27, 33, 41$ and 48 into two sets such that the difference between the sums of the numbers in each of the sets is the least possible.

COMMENTS

Add the numbers and divide their total by 2 or 3 to obtain the sum of the numbers in each set. Then group the numbers, in various ways, to achieve this sum.

Example 1

Put $4, 5, 6, 8, 9$ and 12 into two sets so that each set of numbers has the same total.

$4 + 5 + 6 + 8 + 9 + 12 = 44$

Each set of numbers must total 22 ($44 \div 2$). Examine $4, 5, 6, 8, 9$ and 12 for such a total.

$4 + 6 + 12 = 5 + 8 + 9 = 22$

One set, therefore, contains $4, 6$ and 12; the other contains $5, 8$ and 9.

Example 2

Arrange the numbers $5, 12, 16, 17, 19$ and 24 in two sets so that the difference between the sums of the numbers in each set is the smallest.

$5 + 12 + 16 + 17 + 19 + 24 = 93 \qquad 93 \div 2 = 46\frac{1}{2}$

The least difference between the sums will be 1, when the sets total 46 and 47. Try to obtain these totals, or others nearest to them.

$5 + 17 + 24 = 46 \qquad 12 + 16 + 19 = 47$

One set, therefore, will contain $5, 17$ and 24, and the other $12, 16$ and 19.

N16   *Letters in Words*

(ANSWERS PAGES 151–2)

INVESTIGATIONS

1. Let A = 1, B = 2, C = 3, and so on, up to Z = 26. The value of a word is found by changing its letters into numbers and adding them, e.g. BAD has the value 7 (2 + 1 + 4). Find the values of these animals: cow, cat, dog, pig, lion, deer and bear. Which has the greatest value? Which has the least? Which animals have the same value?

   Can you find any animals with values more than 50 but less than 100?
   Can you find any with values larger than 100? Larger than 150?

2. If A = 1, B = 2, C = 3, and so on, up to Z = 26, find the values of either boys' or girls' first names; for example, Tom has the value 48 (20 + 15 + 13). What names can you find with the greatest and least values?

3. Repeat the procedure of Question 1 finding instead the values of names of birds, garden flowers, wild flowers, trees, rivers or countries.

4. What are the longest and shortest names you can find for a boy, a girl, a kind of tree, a kind of flower, the name of a river or the name of a country?

COMMENTS

Reference books which include lists of first names, birds, animals, flowers, rivers and countries will prove extremely useful. Many other categories, some being suggested by pupils, could also be considered, e.g. breeds of dog, names of fruits, car manufacturers' names.

N17 *Repeated Use of a Digit to Make Prescribed Numbers*

(ANSWERS PAGES 152–3)

FOR INVESTIGATION

1. Using only four 1s, and any of the signs $+$, $-$, $\times$ and $\div$, make all the numbers from 0 to 4 and from 9 to 13. Brackets may also be used, e.g.

$$(1 + 1) \times (1 + 1) = 4 \qquad 11 - (1 \times 1) = 10$$

2. Use five 9s, and any of the signs $+$, $-$, $\times$ and $\div$, to write statements which equal 10. Brackets may also be used, e.g.

$$(99 \div 9) - (9 \div 9) = 10$$

Can you find four more different ways?

3. Use four 5s, arithmetical signs and brackets, to make 25, e.g.

$$(5 \times 5) \times (5 \div 5)$$

Can you find **three** more different ways?

4. Use four 3s, and any of the signs $+$, $-$, $\times$ and $\div$, also brackets, to make all the numbers from 0 to 10 inclusive, e.g.

$$3 + 3 - 3 - 3 = 0 \qquad (33 - 3) \div 3 = 10$$

5. Which of the numbers from 0 to 15, inclusive, can you write using four 7s, brackets, and any of the signs $+$, $-$, $\times$ and $\div$? For example

$$7 + 7 + 7 - 7 = 14$$

6. Which of the numbers from 0 to 10, inclusive, can you write using four 2s, brackets, and any of the signs $+$, $-$, $\times$ and $\div$? For example

$$2 + 2 + 2 - 2 = 4$$

7. Using any of the signs +, −, × and ÷, and brackets, obtain

    (a) 100 using six 9s
    (b) 20 using six 8s
    (c) 140 using six 7s
    (d) 120 using six 6s
    (e) 160 using six 4s

N18 *Find the Number – Digit Sums, Divisibility and Remainders*

(ANSWERS PAGE 153)

FOR SOLUTION

1. Find all two-digit numbers, with digit sums of 8, and which divide exactly by 4.

2. Find all two-digit numbers whose digits add to 7 and which are also prime numbers.

3. The digit sum of a number between 10 and 100 is 7. If the digits are reversed the number obtained is 9 less than the original number. What was the original number?

4. Find the number between 140 and 170 which is odd, divides exactly by 7 and has two digits the same.

5. Find the number between 210 and 230 which divides exactly by 3 and 4 and has a digit sum greater than 10.

6. A number less than 100 divides exactly by 7. When divided by 3 or 8 there is a remainder of 1. What is this number?

7. I have a supply of straws, more than 20 and less than 100. If I arrange them in 3s and make triangles with them, or put them in 4s and make squares with them, I have 2 straws left over each time. What is the least number of straws in the pile for this to happen?
   What other number of straws could be in the pile instead for the same thing to happen?

8. Ian had between 30 and 60 small toy plastic soldiers. When arranged in 2s there was 1 soldier left over, when arranged in 3s there were 2 soldiers left over, and when arranged in 5s there were 4 soldiers left over. How many soldiers did he have?

9. What is the smallest number which leaves a remainder of 1 when divided by 3, a remainder of 3 when divided by 5, and a remainder of 5 when divided by 7?

COMMENTS

Questions of this type often appear clearer to pupils if sequences of numbers are written down and then each number is tested for some other property, or two or more sequences are compared for numbers in common. The writing down process helps pupils to 'see' what is happening and aids their thinking.

Example 1

Find the number between 250 and 300 which divides exactly by 3 and 7 and whose digit sum is less than 10.

Use a calculator to find those numbers between 250 and 300 which divide exactly by 7. Since $250 \div 7 = 35.7$ and $36 \times 7 = 252$, the numbers divisible by 7 are 252, 259, 266, 273, 280, 287 and 294. Which of these divide exactly by 3? Only 252, 273 and 294. Of these, 252 has a digit sum less than 10, so the required number is 252.

Example 2

Find numbers less than 50 which leave a remainder of 1 when divided by 5 and a remainder of 2 when divided by 3.

Numbers which divide exactly by 5 are $5, 10, 15, 20, \ldots, 45$ and 50, so numbers which leave a remainder of 1 when divided by 5 will be one greater than these, namely, $6, 11, 16, 21, 26, 31, 36, 41$ and 46.

Numbers which divide exactly by three are $3, 6, 9, 12, 15, \ldots, 42, 45$ and 48, so numbers which leave a remainder of 2 when divided by 3 will be 2 greater than these, namely, $5, 8, 11, 14, 17, 20, 23, 26, 29, \ldots, 38, 41, 44$ and 47.

On comparing these two sets of numbers we find they both contain 11, 26 and 41, so the required numbers are 11, 26 and 41.

N19 *Making Numbers, Using Given Digits, to Satisfy Prescribed Conditions*

(ANSWERS PAGES 153–4)

FOR INVESTIGATION

1. Use the digits 2, 3, 5 and 7 to make three-digit numbers, the digits chosen being different, e.g. 235, 752. Arrange the numbers in order, greatest to least.

2. Use three different digits, selected from 1, 4, 6 and 7, to make numbers between 100 and 1000, e.g. 641. Arrange these numbers in order, least to greatest.

3. Select three different digits from 2, 4, 5 and 6 and make numbers between 100 and 1000 which divide exactly by 4.

4. Choose any three digits from 3, 4, 7 and 8 and make three-digit numbers which divide exactly by 3. List them, greatest to least.

5. Make three-digit numbers using digits chosen from 1, 2, 3 and 4, such that the digits in each number are all different, and each number does not divide by 3, e.g. 134 or 241. How many different numbers can you find? Arrange them in order.

6. Use the digits 2, 3, 4 and 5 to make three-digit numbers such that no two of the digits add to 6, and the digits in each number are all different. Arrange the numbers in order of size, greatest to least.

7. Make three-digit numbers using digits chosen from 2, 4, 5 and 6, such that the digits in each number are all different and do not add to 12 or 15, e.g. 562. List the numbers in order of size, greatest to least.

8. Use the digits 1, 2, 3, 4 and 5 to make numbers between 100 and 1000, such that no two digits add to 5 or 6, and the digits in each number are all different. Arrange the numbers in order of size, least to greatest.

9. Make three-digit numbers using different digits selected from $1, 2, 3, 4$ and 5, such that no two of the digits add to 4 or 7. How many such numbers can you find?

10. Make three-digit numbers such that no two, or three, of the digits add to 6 or 7, choosing different digits from $1, 2, 3, 4, 5$ and 6. For example, 645 is allowed but 644 is not. How many such numbers can you find?

COMMENTS

Put each of the digits in the hundreds position, in turn, and then arrange the remaining digits in the tens and units places, in order to make various numbers. Having compiled a list of numbers, test each one of them for the property demanded, using a calculator, if necessary.

Example

Use the digits 3, 5, 7 and 9, to make three-digit numbers which divide exactly by 7.

Numbers with 9 in the hundreds position are 975, 973, 957, 953, 937 and 935.
Numbers with 7 in the hundreds position are 795, 793, 759, 753, 739 and 735.
Numbers with 5 in the hundreds position are 597, 593, 579, 573, 539 and 537.
Numbers with 3 in the hundreds position are 397, 395, 379, 375, 359 and 357.

Using a calculator, divide each of these numbers by 7. Those which divide exactly are 973, 735, 539 and 357.

N20 *Obtaining and Making Numbers Using Addition, Subtraction and Multiplication*

(ANSWERS PAGE 154)

1. Use two even numbers and one + sign to produce answers of 28, 36, 48, 64 and 82. Find six different statements for each number, e.g.

    $18 + 10 = 28$, $8 + 20 = 28$,

    and so on.

2. Use two odd numbers and one + sign to produce answers of 26, 34, 48, 56, 68 and 76. Find six different statements for each number, e.g.

    $11 + 15 = 26$, $1 + 25 = 26$,

    and so on.

3. Use three numbers and two + signs to make numbers of 18, 26, 42, 56, 68, 74 and 86. Find four different statements for each. For example,

    $2 + 10 + 6 = 18$, $3 + 6 + 9 = 18$,

    and so on.

4. Use four numbers and three + signs to produce answers of 29, 42, 56, 65, 77 and 89, e.g. $21 + 37 + 5 + 2 = 65$.

5. Use two numbers and one − sign to produce answers of 12, 16, 28 and 32. Find four different statements for each. For example,

    $68 - 56 = 12$, $41 - 29 = 12$,

    and so on.

6. Make up number statements, which include one + sign and one − sign, and produce the numbers $23, 42, 38, 84, 29$ and 65. Can you make each number in three different ways? e.g.

   $75 + 6 - 58 = 23$, $93 - 80 + 10 = 23$, $62 + 35 - 74 = 23$,

   and so on.

7. Use each of the digits $2, 3, 5$ and 7, once only, and two + signs, to make other numbers, e.g. $32 + 5 + 7 = 44$. How many different numbers can you make? Which is greatest? Which is least?

8. Use each of the digits $2, 3$ and 7, and one × sign, to make other numbers, e.g. $23 \times 7 = 161$. Arrange these numbers in order from least to greatest.

9. Use three different digits chosen from $2, 3, 4$ and 5, and one × sign, to make other numbers. What is the greatest number, and the least number, to be made?

10. Use each of the digits $1, 2, 5$ and 6, once only, and one + sign, to make other numbers, e.g. $12 + 56 = 68$, $125 + 6 = 131$. What are the greatest and least numbers which may be made?

11. Use each of the digits $1, 2, 4$ and 5, and one − sign, to make other numbers, e.g. $124 - 5 = 119$, $42 - 15 = 27$. What are the greatest, and least, numbers to be made?

12. Use all the digits $1, 2, 3, 4$ and 5 to make a three-digit number and a two-digit number which have the greatest sum and the least sum. Can you obtain each of these sums in three different ways?

13. Use all the digits $2, 3, 4, 5$ and 6 to make a three-digit number and a two-digit number such that their difference is greatest and their difference is least.

N21 Finding Missing Digits Included in Addition, Subtraction, Multiplication and Division

(ANSWERS PAGES 154–5)

FOR SOLUTION

1. Find the missing numbers.

(a) 64 +
    *8
    ――
    9*

(b) 63 +
    **
    ――
    92

(c) 9* +
    *8
    ――
    *44

(d) 1*7 +
    35*
    ――
    *83

(e) *47 +
    2*7
    ――
    63*

2. Find the missing numbers.

(a) 5* −
    *9
    ――
    28

(b) 7* −
    28
    ――
    *7

(c) ** −
    26
    ――
    43

(d) 8*4 −
    6
    ――
    657

(e) *2* −
    2*8
    ――
    446

3. Find the missing numbers.

(a) 3* ×
    7
    ――
    **8

(b) *6 ×
    6
    ――
    27*

(c) *3 ×
    7
    ――
    0

(d) *** ×
    4
    ――
    532

(e) 156 ×
    *
    ――
    468

4. Find the missing numbers.

(a) 4)91*
    **8

(b) 3)*22
    27*

(c) 4)*2*
    132

(d) 5)7**
    *49

(e) 3)***
    156

COMMENTS

Questions 1 and 2 require a full knowledge of addition and subtraction facts to 20, whilst questions 3 and 4 need multiplication tables and division facts.

N22 Number Relationships Including Missing Numbers

(ANSWERS PAGE 155)

FOR SOLUTION

Find the missing numbers indicated by asterisks in the following questions.

1.
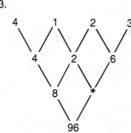

2.
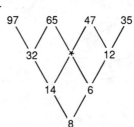

3.

4.

5.
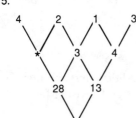

6.
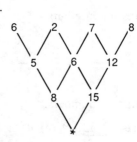

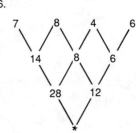

N23 *Addition with Letters Replacing Digits*

(ANSWERS PAGES 155–6)

TO BE SOLVED

1. Find A, B and C, all different digits, such that

$$
\begin{array}{r}
AB\ + \\
AB \\
\underline{AB} \\
BC
\end{array}
$$

2. Find A, B and C, all different digits, such that

$$
\begin{array}{r}
AB\ + \\
AB \\
\underline{AB} \\
CA
\end{array}
$$

3. Find A, B and C, all different digits, such that

$$
\begin{array}{r}
AB\ + \\
AB \\
AB \\
\underline{AB} \\
CA
\end{array}
$$

4. A, B and C represent different digits. Find them if

$$
\begin{array}{r}
AB\ + \\
AB \\
AB \\
\underline{AB} \\
CBA
\end{array}
$$

5.   Find A, B and C, all different digits, such that

$$
\begin{array}{r}
AB + \\
AB \\
AB \\
\hline
CCC
\end{array}
$$

6.   Find A, B and C, all different digits, such that

$$
\begin{array}{r}
ABC + \\
ABC \\
ABC \\
\hline
CCC
\end{array}
$$

7.   Find A, B, C and D, if different digits, such that

$$
\begin{array}{r}
ABC + \\
ABC \\
\hline
DCA
\end{array}
$$

8.   Find A, B, C and D; if they are all different digits chosen from 1, 2, 3, 4, 5, 6, 7, 8 and 9, such that

$$
\begin{array}{r}
ABC + \\
CBA \\
\hline
DDD
\end{array}
$$

9.   Find O, N, E, T and W, if these letters have different values selected from 1, 2, 3, 4, 5, 6, 7, 8 and 9, such that

$$
\begin{array}{r}
ONE + \\
ONE \\
\hline
TWO
\end{array}
$$

Can you find six different solutions?

10.   Put all the digits from 1 to 9 in the sum

$$
\begin{array}{r}
*** + \\
*** \\
\hline
***
\end{array}
$$

Can you find ten or more different solutions?

COMMENTS

The following hints may prove useful.

Questions 1-7

Let each of the digits from 1 to 9, in turn, represent the *units* letter of the number. The units letter of the answer can then be found and sometimes inserted in other positions. The remaining digits can then be allocated to other letters, and tested.

Question 8

There is no carrying from hundreds to thousands so $A + C$ is 9 or less. This indicates there is also no carrying from units to tens. $A + C = D$ in both units and hundreds columns so there is no carrying from tens to hundreds and B is 4 or less. If $B + B = D$, possible values are $B = 1$ with $D = 2$, $B = 2$ with $D = 4$, $B = 3$ with $D = 6$, or $B = 4$ with $D = 8$. Enter these values in the sum, in turn, and then consider possible values for A and C which satisfy $A + C = 2, 4, 6$ and 8.

Question 9

Notice that O must be 4 or less because there is no carrying from hundreds to thousands. Let E = 1, 2, 3, 4, ..., 8 and 9, in turn, and find possible values of O and T. Note that should O = 3 then T may be 6 or 7. Write down the addition with possible values for E, O and T inserted and from the remaining digits, in each case, choose suitable values for N and W.

Question 10

Select three digits which make an addition less than 10, put them in either the units or hundreds position, and see whether the remaining digits may occupy the empty spaces. Suppose we use 1, 7 and 8 as units because $1 + 7 = 8$.

$$\begin{array}{ccc} **1\ + & *91\ + & 291\ + \\ **7 & *57 & 357 \\ \hline **8 & *48 & 648 \end{array}$$

This leaves 2, 3, 4, 5, 6 and 9 for the hundreds and tens. If carrying takes place in the tens column these digits may all be utilized with $9 + 5 = 10 + 4$ and $2 + 3 + 1 = 6$, in the tens and hundreds as shown above.

The placing of the digits may then be varied to provide other possible solutions.

$$\begin{array}{cccc} 291\ + & 297\ + & 257\ + & 251\ + \\ 357 & 351 & 391 & 397 \\ \hline 648 & 648 & 648 & 648 \end{array}$$

The units column may also be moved to form a new hundreds column.

$$\begin{array}{cccc} 129\ + & 729\ + & 725\ + & 125\ + \\ 735 & 135 & 139 & 739 \\ \hline 864 & 864 & 864 & 864 \end{array}$$

This approach may be used to find some other solutions.

N24   *All Digits One Out*

(ANSWERS PAGE 156)

FOR SOLUTION

In these questions, and answers, every digit is either one greater or one less than its true value. Find the correct questions and answers.

1. $\begin{array}{r} 19\ + \\ 34 \\ \hline 80 \end{array}$	2. $\begin{array}{r} 90\ + \\ 27 \\ \hline 86 \end{array}$	3. $\begin{array}{r} 94\ - \\ 30 \\ \hline 71 \end{array}$	4. $\begin{array}{r} 43\ - \\ 34 \\ \hline 42 \end{array}$
5. $\begin{array}{r} 81\ - \\ 20 \\ \hline 92 \end{array}$	6. $\begin{array}{r} 28\ \times \\ 4 \\ \hline 274 \end{array}$	7. $\begin{array}{r} 28\ \times \\ 5 \\ \hline 257 \end{array}$	8. $\begin{array}{r} 36\ \times \\ 4 \\ \hline 250 \end{array}$
9. $\begin{array}{r} 65\ \times \\ 4 \\ \hline 253 \end{array}$	10. $\begin{array}{r} 72\ \times \\ 3 \\ \hline 361 \end{array}$	11. $\begin{array}{r} 4)\underline{823} \\ 353 \end{array}$	12. $\begin{array}{r} 4)\underline{716} \\ 234 \end{array}$

COMMENTS

Substitute the possible true number values in the questions and work them out. Then compare their answers with the incorrect answer. An answer with all its digits 'one out' is the true one. This procedure is best illustrated with a worked out question.

Example

If $23 \times 5 = 219$, and all the digits are 'one out', find the correct question and answer.

   The true value of the 23 could be $14, 34, 12$ or 32, while the true value of the multiplier could be 4 or 6.

The correct multiplication question and its answer could be

14 ×	34 ×	12 ×	32 ×	14 ×	34 ×	12 ×	32 ×
4	4	4	4	6	6	6	6
56	136	48	128	84	204	72	192

Comparing each of these answers with 219 we find that 128 has all its digits 'one out'. Therefore, $32 \times 4 = 128$ is the correct question and answer.

The included addition, subtraction and division questions could be tackled in a similar manner.

N25 *Involving Prime Numbers*

(ANSWERS PAGES 156–7)

INVESTIGATIONS

1. How many factors has each of the numbers from 1 to 30, inclusive? For example, 27 has four factors: 1, 3, 9 and 27. Which numbers have only two factors? Which numbers have an odd number of factors? Which numbers have six factors? Which numbers have eight factors?

2. Find prime numbers less than 100.

3. Find prime numbers, less than 100, which are

   (a) one more than a perfect square,
   (b) one less than a perfect square, and
   (c) one less than a perfect cube.

4. House numbers on one side of a road are all odd and go from 1 to 79 inclusive. Among them is a terrace of 5 houses, the middle house having a prime number whilst the others do not. Find the house numbers.

5. Obtain a list of prime numbers less than 50. Use this list to express each of the numbers from 5 to 50, inclusive, as the sum of two different prime numbers. Which numbers cannot be written in this way?

6. Obtain a list of prime numbers less than 150. From it choose four different numbers, each less than 50, and find their sum. Then try to obtain, from the list, the same sum using three different, then two different, prime numbers, e.g.

   $$11 + 13 + 17 + 41 = 82 \qquad 2 + 37 + 43 = 82 \qquad 11 + 71 = 82$$

7. Make four prime numbers using all the digits 1, 2, 3, 4, 5, 6 and 7, each once only.

COMMENTS

Question 1 develops the meaning of the word 'factor' and suggests that numbers have not, necessarily, the same number of them. Numbers such as 2, 3, 7, 11 and 13 have only two distinct factors and are prime. One is *not* prime because it has only one factor. Numbers with three or more factors are rectangular, and also possibly square, because they may be represented by rectangular patterns of dots, e.g. 16 or 18. Prime numbers will not make rectangular dot patterns.

Question 2 concerns the finding of primes up to 100. This may be assisted by writing the numbers from 1 to 100 on a 10 by 10 number square, and crossing out 1, every second number after two, every third number after three, every fourth number after four, every fifth number after five, and so on. Talk about those numbers which have been crossed out and those which have not. Check those not crossed out against a list of primes. Who devised this method for finding primes? (It is called the Sieve of Eratosthenes.)

Lists of prime numbers, up to 150, may be consulted when gaining solutions to questions 3–7.

N26 *Continuing Sequences*

(ANSWERS PAGE 157)

Find the next three numbers in order to continue each of the following sequences.

1. $5, 8, 11, 14, 17, 20, 23, \ldots, \ldots, \ldots$

2. $1, 8, 15, 22, 29, 36, 43, \ldots, \ldots, \ldots$

3. $2, 13, 24, 35, 46, 57, 68, \ldots, \ldots, \ldots$

4. $1, 2, 4, 8, 16, 32, \ldots, \ldots, \ldots$

5. $1, 2, 3, 5, 8, 13, 21, \ldots, \ldots, \ldots$

6. $1, 4, 9, 16, 25, 36, 49, \ldots, \ldots, \ldots$

7. $1, 3, 6, 10, 15, 21, 28, \ldots, \ldots, \ldots$

8. $3, 5, 8, 12, 17, 23, 30, \ldots, \ldots, \ldots$

9. $1, 2, 5, 10, 17, 26, 37, \ldots, \ldots, \ldots$

10. $3, 6, 11, 18, 27, 38, 51, \ldots, \ldots, \ldots$

11. $4, 11, 22, 37, 56, 79, 106, \ldots, \ldots, \ldots$

12. $1, 7, 19, 37, 61, 91, 127, \ldots, \ldots, \ldots$

13. $1, 11, 27, 49, 77, 111, 151, \ldots, \ldots, \ldots$

14. $2, 5, 11, 23, 47, 95, \ldots, \ldots, \ldots$

COMMENTS

In a sequence, find whether each number

(a) is larger or smaller than the previous one by a fixed amount, e.g. 3 more as in 5, 8, 11, 14, 17, ...
(b) is larger or smaller than the previous one by a constant ratio, e.g. 3 times larger as in 2, 6, 18, 54, 162, ...
(c) is obtained by adding two previous terms as in 2, 4, 6, 10, 16, 26, 42, 68, ...

If none of these ideas are fruitful then consider the use of differences.

Example

Find the next three numbers in the sequence 9, 14, 21, 30, 41, 54, ...

	9	14	21	30	41	54	*	*	*
1st differences		5	7	9	11	13	*	*	*
2nd differences			2	2	2	2	*	*	*

Fig. 1.35

Knowing that 2nd differences are all 2 (Fig. 1.35), enables 1st differences to be extended (15, 17, 19) and these numbers allow the sequence to be continued. The next three terms are 69 (54 + 15), 86 (69 + 17) and 105 (86 + 19).

N27 *Pattern and Prediction*

(ANSWERS PAGES 157–8)

ACTIVITIES

1. Find the number of different ways from A to B in each of the diagrams shown in Fig. 1.36 if travel is only allowed along the lines, to the right or down, and record them in sequence. How many different ways from A to B will there be in the 20th shape of the series?

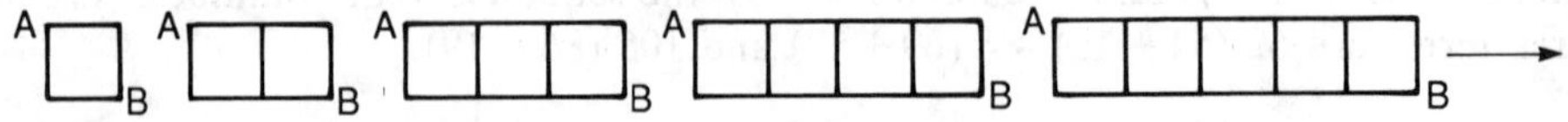

Fig. 1.36

2. The shapes shown in Fig. 1.37 are made with matchsticks. How many match-sticks are there in each shape? Write down a sequence which describes how the number of matchsticks grows as the shapes get larger. How many matchsticks will there be in the 15th shape?

Fig. 1.37

3. The shapes shown in Fig. 1.38 are made with matchsticks. Find the number of matchsticks in the perimeter of each shape. Write down a sequence which shows how the perimeters grow for the first 5 shapes. How many matchsticks will there be in the perimeter of the 12th shape if the same pattern of growth is continued?

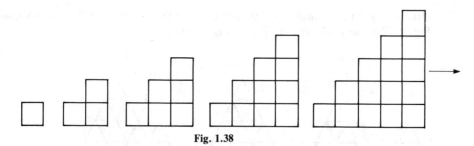

Fig. 1.38

4. Write down a number sequence which shows how the perimeters of the shapes, shown in Fig. 1.39, grow if they are made with matchsticks. How many matchsticks will there be in the perimeter of the 10th shape for this pattern of growth?

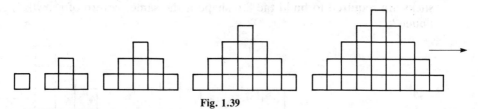

Fig. 1.39

5. The shapes shown in Fig. 1.40 are made with matchsticks. Write down a sequence which shows how the perimeters of the shapes grow. How many matchsticks will there be in the perimeter of the 13th shape for this growth?

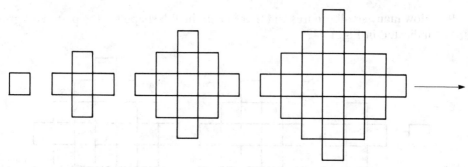

Fig. 1.40

6. How many squares are there in each of the shapes shown in Fig. 1.41? Write these numbers in sequence to show how the number of squares grow. How many different squares will there be in the 17th shape for this growth?

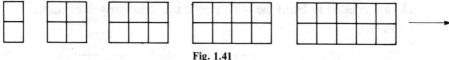

Fig. 1.41

7. How many small triangles will there be in the 8th diagram of the series shown in Fig. 1.42 if the same growth pattern is continued?

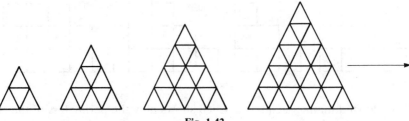

Fig. 1.42

8. The shapes shown in Fig. 1.43 are made with matchsticks. How many matchsticks are required to build the 8th shape if the same pattern of growth is continued?

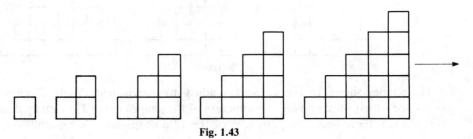

Fig. 1.43

9. How many small squares will there be in the 9th shape for the pattern of growth indicated in Fig. 1.44?

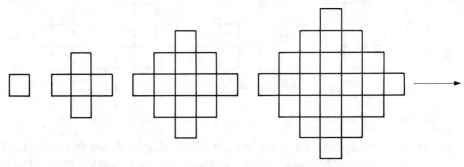

Fig. 1.44

10. The shapes shown in Fig. 1.45 are made with matchsticks. How many matchsticks are needed to build the 8th shape if the same growth continues?

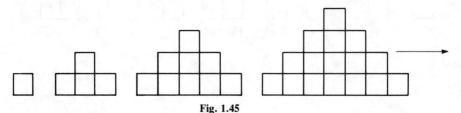

Fig. 1.45

11. Find the number of different rectangles in each of the diagrams shown in Fig. 1.46, record them, and then find the number of rectangles in the 10th shape if the same growth pattern is continued.

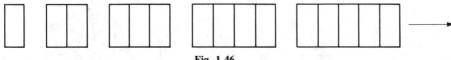

Fig. 1.46

12. Record the number of straight lines needed to join up points arranged roughly in a circle. Each point must be joined to every other point as in Fig. 1.47. Write down a sequence which describes how the number of lines grows. How many lines are needed to join 12 points placed on a circle?

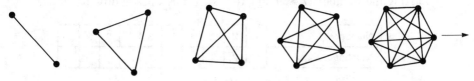

Fig. 1.47

13. Fourteen people go to a meeting. Each one shakes hands with everyone else. How many handshakes were made altogether?

To answer this question consider the number of handshakes for 2, 3, 4, 5 and 6 people and record these results. A pattern may then be seen to develop which could be extended.

14. Find the number of ways along the lines from P to Q in each of the diagrams shown in Fig. 1.48, travelling only to the right or down, and record them in a sequence. How many different ways from P to Q will there be in the 10th diagram for this particular pattern of growth?

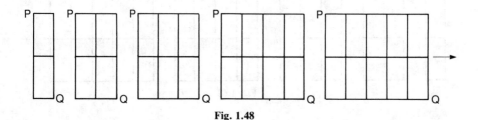

Fig. 1.48

15. Draw polygons with 4, 5, 6, 7 and 8 sides. Draw all the diagonals in each, as shown in Fig. 1.49, and record these results in sequence. How many diagonals could be drawn in a decagon, a ten-sided polygon? Could a polygon have 55 diagonals?

Fig. 1.49

16. Obtain a Colour Factor or Cuisenaire set. Using *only* ones and twos build the numbers from 1 to 6, inclusive, in as many different ways as possible. Enter the results in a table as shown in Fig. 1.50. How many different ways are there of making the numbers 7, 8, 9 and 10, using only ones and twos?

Number	1	2	3	4	5	6	7	8	9	10
Number of ways	1	2	3							

Fig. 1.50

17. Divide a circle with 1, 2, 3, 4 and 5 straight lines, into the *greatest* number of possible parts. Record the results in a table as shown in Fig. 1.51. What is the maximum number of parts a circle may be divided into, with 10 straight lines?

Number of lines	1	2	3	4	5	6	7	8	9	10
Number of parts	2	4								

18. Find the number of rectangles in each of the shapes shown in Fig. 1.52. Use these results to predict the number of rectangles in the 8th shape if the same pattern of growth is continued.

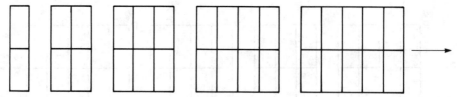

Fig. 1.52

19. How many different squares are there in each of the diagrams shown in Fig. 1.53. Use these results to predict the number of squares in the 8th diagram if the same growth pattern is continued.

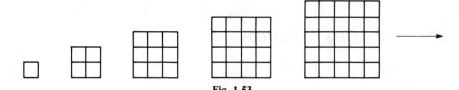

Fig. 1.53

COMMENTS

Ensure that the pupils are able to extend sequences before attempting these questions. Should guidance be needed, refer to the section 'Continuing Sequences'.

N28   *Various Games*

(ANSWERS PAGE 159)

1. Find the least number of moves, moving only one counter at a time, to change each of the triangles shown in Fig. 1.54 from left-facing to right-facing.

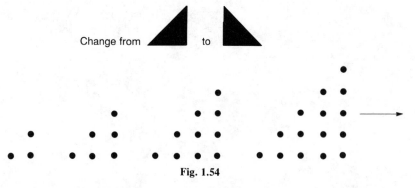

Fig. 1.54

Investigate for the first 7 triangles of the series and record the number of moves as shown in Fig. 1.55.

Triangle number	1st	2nd	3rd	4th	5th	6th	7th
Number of moves							

Fig. 1.55

2. There are 7 black counters and 1 white counter on a nine-square grid as shown in Fig. 1.56. The aim is to move the white counter into the empty space in the opposite corner. Counters can move up, down or sideways, but *not* diagonally, into an *empty* adjacent space. What is the least number of moves to make this possible?

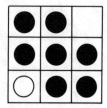

Fig. 1.56

3. Black and white counters, 10 of each colour, are placed alternately, black, white, black, white, etc., in a row on a 20-square grid as shown in Fig. 1.57. By exchanging *adjacent* counters *only*, the objective is to arrange all the white counters together on the left side and all the black ones together on the right. What is the least number of moves needed to do this?

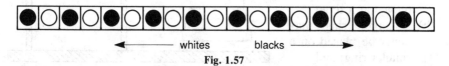

Fig. 1.57

(Hint: attempt this game first with a smaller number of counters, such as 2 (black, white), then 4 (black, white, black, white), then 6 (black, white, black, white, black, white), and so on, recording the number of moves required. Is there an emerging pattern which enables a prediction to be made for 10 white and 10 black counters?)

4. What is the least number of moves needed to replace the 8 black counters with the 8 white counters in Fig. 1.58, if any counter can only slide into an empty adjacent space or jump over one counter of another colour to an empty adjacent space?

Fig. 1.58

(Note: perform this task with smaller grids and fewer counters, e.g. 1 white and 1 black on a 3-grid, 2 white and 2 black on a 5-grid, and so on, recording the number of moves needed. A prediction may be possible for larger numbers of counters.)

5. What is the least number of moves needed to replace the row of 20 white counters with the row of 20 black counters shown in Fig. 1.59, if any counter can only be moved across, up, down or diagonally, to an empty adjacent square?

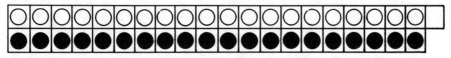

Fig. 1.59

(At first, play the game with fewer counters on smaller grids, e.g. 1 black and 1 white on a 3-grid, 2 black and 2 white on a 5-grid, and so on, recording the number of moves needed. Is there an emerging pattern?)

6. Seven rings placed on spike A of a 'Tower of Hanoi' (Fig. 1.60) are to be moved to spike C according to these rules:

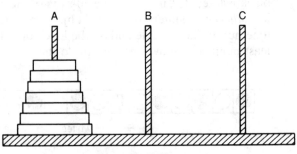

Fig. 1.60

   (a) only one ring may be moved at a time;
   (b) a larger ring may never be placed on a smaller ring; and
   (c) all three spikes may be used.

   What is the least number of moves needed to rebuild the tower on spike C? (Hint: obtain a 'Tower of Hanoi' and perform the task using fewer rings on spike A, recording the results each time, e.g. 2 rings, 3 rings, 4 rings, and so on. A prediction may then be possible.)

N29 *A Thousands Mixture*

(ANSWERS PAGE 159)

INVESTIGATIONS

1. Use all the digits 1, 3, 6 and 8, each once only, to make numbers larger than 1000. Arrange these numbers in order, greatest to least.

2. Use the digits 4, 5, 6 and 9 to make numbers larger than 1000, the digits in each number being different. Arrange these numbers in order, greatest to least.

3. Use all the digits 2, 3, 5, 7 and 9 to make a three-digit number and a two-digit number which have the greatest sum, and the least sum.

4. Use all the digits 1, 2, 3, 4, 7 and 8, to make two three-digit numbers which have the greatest and least sums.

5. Find the missing digits in the following questions.

(a)
```
 *5*4 +
 5*5*
 ────
 9181
```
(b)
```
  4* +
  9*3
 ────
 **21
```
(c)
```
 24* ×
   7
 ────
 ***1
```
(d)
```
 3*6 ×
   4
 ────
 *42*
```

6. In the given multiplication questions, each digit is either one greater or one less than its true value. Find the correct questions and answers.

(a)
```
 132 ×
   4
 ────
 2126
```
(b)
```
 525 ×
   3
 ────
 1445
```

COMMENTS

These types of question have been included earlier in the text but with numbers less than 1000. Those in this section involve thousands. Refer back, if necessary, to the comments included in the following sections.

N19   Making numbers, using given digits, to satisfy prescribed conditions.

N21   Finding missing digits included in addition, subtraction, multiplication and division.

N24   All digits one out.

N30 *Finding, with a Calculator, Those Numbers Which Divide Exactly by their Digit Sums*

(ANSWERS PAGE 160)

FOR INVESTIGATION

1. Find three-digit numbers which divide exactly by 15 and whose digits add to 15. For example: 465, because $465 \div 15 = 31$ and $4 + 6 + 5 = 15$. Can you find twelve more such numbers?

2. The number 156 divides exactly by 12 and its digits add to 12. Can you find eight more numbers between 100 and 500 with this property?

3. Find three-digit numbers which divide exactly by 6 and whose digits add to 6. There are twelve such numbers.

4. Find numbers between 100 and 1000 which divide exactly by 17 and whose digits add to 17, e.g. 629.

5. Find three-digit numbers which divide exactly by 13 and whose digits add to 13, e.g. 247.

6. Are there any numbers less than 1000 which divide exactly by 19 and whose digits also add to 19?

7. Some numbers between 1000 and 5000 divide exactly by 23 and their digits add to 23, e.g. 1886. Can you find six more such numbers?

COMMENTS

The method of solution used may be similar to that illustrated in the following example.

Example

Find three-digit numbers less than 400 which divide exactly by 14 and whose digits add to 14.

Since $100 \div 14 = 7.1$ and $14 \times 8 = 112$, to find multiples of 14 between 100 and 400, start at 112 and keep adding on 14, recording the numbers obtained.

112   126   140   154   168   182   196   210   224   238   252
266   280   294   308   322   336   350   364   378   392

Add the digits of each and see if any total 14. Two numbers, 266 and 392, meet this requirement.

The list of multiples need not be written down, since the digits of each new number displayed on the calculator could be added mentally as successive fourteens are added to 112. Those numbers with digit sums of fourteen could then be noted, as the adding continues. Check the numbers obtained for errors.

N31 *Multiplication Involving the Use of a Calculator*

(ANSWERS PAGES 160–1)

INVESTIGATIONS

1. What is the greatest number you can produce using the digits 1, 2, 3 and 4, and one × sign? For example, $314 \times 2 = 628$, $13 \times 24 = 312$, and so on.

2. Make different numbers using the digits 1, 2, 3 and 5, and one × sign, each once only. For example, $51 \times 23 = 1173$, $531 \times 2 = 1062$, and so on. Which statements produce the greatest and least numbers?

3. A rectangle is twice as long as it is wide and its area is 3698 sq. cm. Find its length and breadth.

4. A rectangle is three times longer than it is wide and its area is 9075 sq. cm. Find its length and breadth.

5. Find two consecutive numbers which have a product of 3192, and three consecutive numbers which have a product of 19656.

6. Use the digits 1, 3, 4, 5 and 6 to make a three-digit number and a two-digit number such that their product is greatest. Repeat the procedure to obtain the least product.

7. Use the digits 1, 2, 3, 4, 5 and 6 to make three two-digit numbers which when multiplied together provide the greatest and least answers.

8. Use the digits 1, 2, 3, 4, 5 and 6 to make two three-digit numbers such that the products obtained are greatest and least.

9. Use all the digits 2, 3, 4, 5, 6 and 7 to make two three-digit numbers which when multiplied produce the greatest and least answers.

10. Find two square numbers which have a sum of 1405. Can you find two answers?

11. Small tins of fruit cost 25p each and large tins cost 49p each. If the tins sold amount exactly to £20, how many large and small tins were bought?

COMMENTS

The following remarks may prove helpful.

Questions 1, 2, 7–9

Use the given digits and compile a list of various numbers and the calculations to be performed. Use a calculator to obtain their answers and record them. Greatest and least values may then be found.

Questions 3, 4, 5

Use trial and improvement: e.g. find two consecutive numbers whose product is 1482

$17 \times 18 = 306$	Too small
$27 \times 28 = 756$	Too small
$37 \times 38 = 1406$	Too small
$38 \times 39 = 1482$	Just right

Pupils also need to know that the area of a rectangle equals its length multiplied by breadth.

Question 10

A list of square numbers need to be compiled and consulted, up to 37×37: $1, 4, 9, 16, \ldots, 1369$.

Question 11

Examine the tens and units digits of numbers which are multiples of 25. What do you notice? Build up multiples of 49, using a calculator, and see if these number endings are attainable.

N32 *Involving Palindromes*

(ANSWERS PAGE 161)

FOR CONSIDERATION

1. A number such as 14341 is called a palindrome. That is, it reads the same from left to right as from right to left.

   Find and write down all palindromes with three digits, e.g. 262 and 585. How many three-digit numbers are palindromes? Also find four-digit numbers which are palindromes.

2. The date 28 January 1982 is palindromic if written as 28–1–82, and 28 November 1982 is also the palindromic date of 28–11–82. 1983, however, has no palindromic dates. Why not?

   Write down all the palindromic dates for 1991. How many more palindromic dates will occur before the year 2000?

3. Add the reverse of any number to itself, repeatedly, until a palindromic number is obtained, recording the number of steps required for this to happen.

274		
472		
746	not a palindrome	(1st step)
647		
1393	not a palindrome	(2nd step)
3931		
5324	not a palindrome	(3rd step)
4235		
9559	a palindrome	(4th step)

   So starting with 274, four steps are needed to produce a palindrome. Now repeat this with the numbers 29, 1725, 85, 67, 371, 329, 179, 796, 376 and 678.

   Can you find a number, or numbers, which need five or more steps to provide a palindrome? A calculator may be used.

N33 *Finding Numbers with Particular Properties*

(ANSWERS PAGES 161–2)

FOR INVESTIGATION

1. Many numbers can be written as the sum of two or more consecutive numbers:

    $5 = 2 + 3 \qquad 18 = 5 + 6 + 7 \qquad 10 = 1 + 2 + 3 + 4$

    Which numbers from 3 to 50, inclusive, can be written as the sum of consecutive numbers and which ones cannot?

2. Which numbers from 1 to 50 have an odd number of factors? For example, 15 divides exactly by $1, 3, 5$ and 15, and has 4 factors, an even number. Use your findings to predict which numbers between 50 and 100 may have an odd number of factors. Check these predictions.

3. Find all three-digit numbers which when 'reversed', and subtracted, provide a difference of 495. For example, 823 'reversed' gives 328, and $823 - 328 = 495$. How many such numbers have this property? (The numbers 520 and 580 would produce 025 and 085 on 'reversal'. Numbers, such as these, which produce 'reversal' numbers with leading zeros are not, in this case, counted.)

4. 756 is a three-digit number which when 'reversed' gives 657. Now $756 - 657 = 99$. Find all the numbers between 100 and 1000 which when 'reversed' produce a difference of 99. How many such numbers are there? (Ignore numbers making 'reversals' with leading zeros, e.g. 130 or 150.)

5. The number 412 when 'reversed' gives 214. The difference between 412 and 214 is 198. 198, added to its 'reverse' 891 makes 1089.

$$
\begin{array}{r}
412\ - \\
\underline{214} \\
198\ + \\
\underline{891} \\
1089
\end{array}
$$

Find all three-digit numbers, less than 500, which following the procedure just described produce 1089. How many such numbers are there? (Numbers such as 260 and 280 which produce 'reversals' with leading zeros are not to be counted.)

COMMENTS

Question 1

Evaluate

$1 + 2$	$2 + 3$	$3 + 4$	$4 + 5$	...
$1 + 2 + 3$	$2 + 3 + 4$	$3 + 4 + 5$	$4 + 5 + 6$	...
$1 + 2 + 3 + 4$	$2 + 3 + 4 + 5$	$3 + 4 + 5 + 6$	$4 + 5 + 6 + 7$	...
$1 + 2 + 3 + 4 + 5$	$2 + 3 + 4 + 5 + 6$	$3 + 4 + 5 + 6 + 7$	...	...

and so on, until 50 is passed. Those numbers not obtained cannot be written as consecutive sums.

Question 2

Use a calculator to perform the necessary divisions.

Question 3

Numbers which produce differences of 495 have a hundreds digit which is 5 greater than its units digit, e.g. 934, 722, 631. List all such numbers.

Question 4

Numbers which produce 99 differences have a hundreds digit that is 1 greater than its units digit, e.g. 928, 766, 493. List all such numbers.

Question 5

Find numbers which produce differences of 198 and 297 on 'reversal'.

Shape and Space Activities

S1 *Matchstick Puzzles*

(ANSWERS PAGE 165)

ACTIVITIES

1. Nine matchsticks are arranged as shown in Fig. 2.1.
    Remove

    (a) 2 matchsticks to leave only 3 triangles
    (b) 3 matchsticks to leave only 2 triangles
    (c) 3 matchsticks to leave only 1 triangle
    (d) 1 matchstick to leave only 3 triangles
    (e) 2 matchsticks to leave only 2 triangles

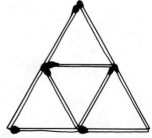

Fig. 2.1

2. Arrange 12 matchsticks as shown in Fig. 2.2.
    Remove

    (a) 2 matchsticks so that only 3 squares remain
    (b) 4 matchsticks so that only 2 squares remain
    (c) 1 matchstick so that only 3 squares remain
    (d) 2 matchsticks so that only 2 squares remain

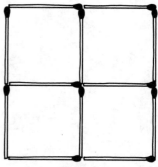

Fig. 2.2

3. Fifteen matchsticks are arranged
    as shown in Fig. 2.3.
    Remove

    (a) 1 matchstick so that only 4
    squares remain
    (b) 3 matchsticks so that only 3
    squares remain
    (c) 5 matchsticks so that only 3
    squares remain
    (d) 4 matchsticks so that only 2
    squares remain
    (e) 2 matchsticks so that only 3
    squares remain

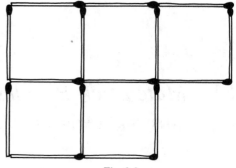

Fig. 2.3

S2 *Finding Given Shapes within Various Diagrams*

(ANSWERS PAGE 165)

FOR INVESTIGATION

1. How many different triangles are there in each of the diagrams shown in Fig. 2.4?

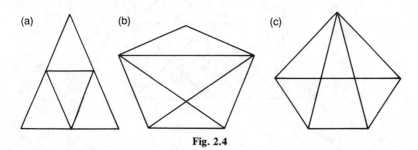

(a)   (b)   (c)

Fig. 2.4

2. How many different quadrilaterals are there in Fig. 2.5?

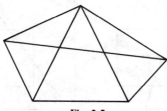

Fig. 2.5

3. How many different rectangles are there in each of the shapes given in Fig. 2.6?

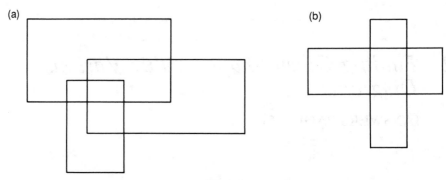

Fig. 2.6

4. How many different squares are there in Fig. 2.7?

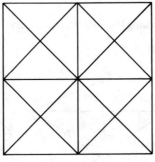

Fig. 2.7

5. How many different triangles, quadrilaterals and pentagons are there in each of the diagrams shown in Fig. 2.8?

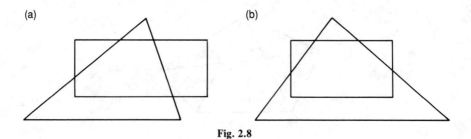

Fig. 2.8

6. How many different triangles are there in each diagram of Fig. 2.9?

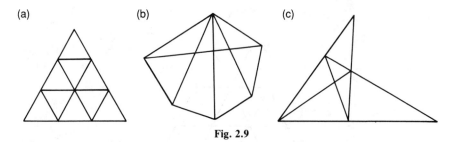

(a) (b) (c)

Fig. 2.9

7. How many different squares are there in Fig. 2.10?

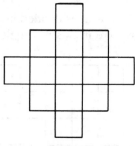

Fig. 2.10

8. How many different triangles are there in each diagram of Fig. 2.11?

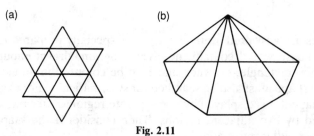

(a) (b)

Fig. 2.11

9. How many different rectangles are there in each diagram of Fig. 2.12?

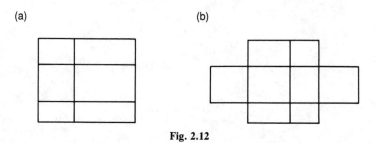

(a) (b)

Fig. 2.12

10. How many different triangles are there in Fig. 2.13?

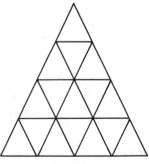

Fig. 2.13

11. A rectangle 6 cm long and 3 cm wide is divided into 18 squares of side 1 cm as in Fig. 2.14. How many squares are in this rectangle?

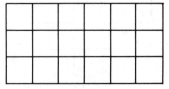

Fig. 2.14

COMMENTS

These questions are answered more effectively if specially prepared recording sheets are available. These would contain the given diagram, drawn enough times, for a different triangle, rectangle, or other shape, to be coloured in on each diagram.

The required shape must also be searched for systematically. For example, colour in the required shape if it is displayed by one separate region. After this see whether the shape is formed by two adjacent regions. Then consider if the shape is formed by 3, 4, 5, and so on, adjacent regions.

S3 *Drawing Given Shapes on Square Dot Lattice Paper*

(ANSWERS PAGE 166)

INVESTIGATIONS

1. How many different-shaped triangles can be made by joining dots on a 9-dot lattice? See Fig. 2.15. Every triangle must have a dot at each corner.

Fig. 2.15

2. How many different-shaped triangles can be made by joining dots within an 8-dot lattice? See Fig. 2.16. All triangles must have a dot in each corner.

Fig. 2.16

3. How many squares can be drawn within the 9-dot lattice shown in Fig. 2.15 if a dot must be in every corner of each square?

4. Draw 10 different hexagons in a 12-dot lattice. See Fig. 2.17. Each shape must have a dot at every corner.

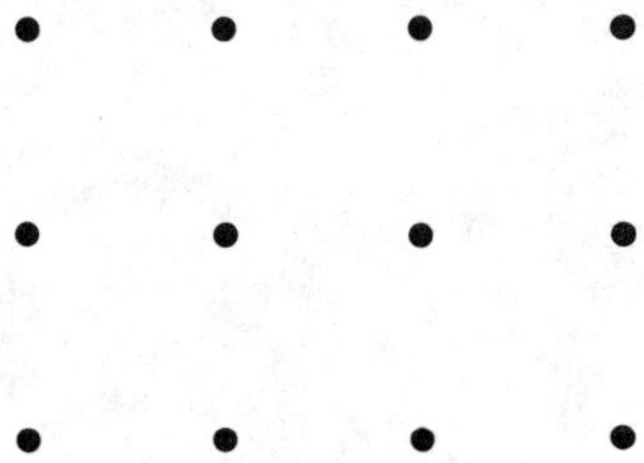

Fig. 2.17

5. How many different-shaped hexagons, with a dot at each corner, can be drawn on a 9-dot lattice? See Fig. 2.15.

6. How many different-shaped quadrilaterals can be formed by joining dots on the 9-dot lattice shown in Fig. 2.15? Each quadrilateral must have a dot in every corner.

7. How many different-shaped pentagons, with a dot in each corner, can be drawn on the 9-dot lattice of Fig. 2.15?

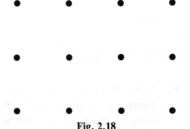

8. How many squares can be drawn in a 16-dot lattice? See Fig. 2.18. Every square must have a dot at each corner.

Fig. 2.18

COMMENTS

These investigations would be answered by drawing the shapes on square dot-lattice paper.

The pupils should, in some of these questions, be sure that the presented shapes are different. This means that a rotation or reflection of a shape is not allowed because the same shape is produced. The question 'How many squares can be drawn?', however, does allow the same shape to be presented in different positions.

S4 *Different Routes*

(ANSWERS PAGE 166)

FOR INVESTIGATION

1. There are three different roads from Tom's house to Jeff's house, and two different ways from Jeff's house to Barry's house as shown in Fig. 2.19. How many different ways are there from Tom's house to Barry's house if, on the way, he calls for Jeff?

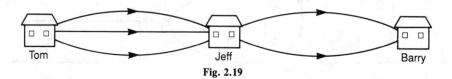

Fig. 2.19

2. Sue calls for Jill and Margaret on the way to school. The possible roads between Sue's house and school are shown in Fig. 2.20. How many different possible ways are there for Sue to travel to school if she follows the roads in the directions indicated?

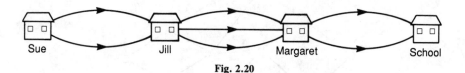

Fig. 2.20

3. In how many ways can the word MATHS be read from left to right in Fig. 2.21 if each letter connects with its neighbour along one of the marked lines?

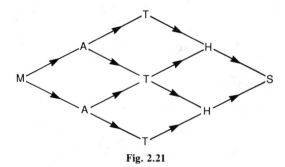

Fig. 2.21

4. In the diagrams shown in Fig. 2.22, how many different ways can be taken from A to B if roads are followed only in the directions indicated?

(a)   (b)   (c)

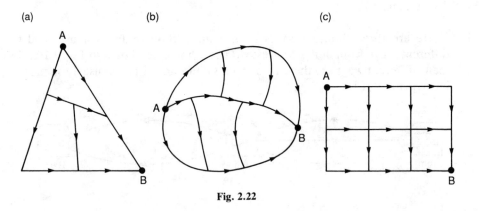

Fig. 2.22

5. In how many ways can the word SQUARE be read from left to right in Fig. 2.23, if each letter connects with its neighbour along one of the marked lines?

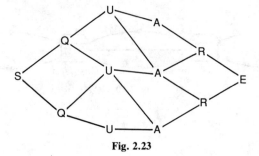

Fig. 2.23

6. You wish to travel from A to B (Fig. 2.24) using only the roads shown in the given directions. How many different possible routes are there?

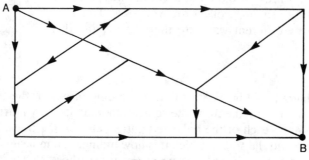

Fig. 2.24

7. How many different ways from A to B in Fig. 2.25 if only the roads shown, in the given directions, are used?

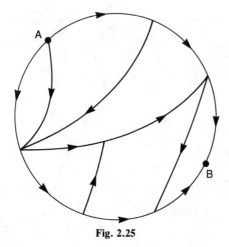

Fig. 2.25

8. Start at the central letter, T, of Fig. 2.26. Move from square to square across, up or down, but *not* diagonally, and collect the letters I, M and E, in that order, to form the word TIME.

How many different ways can you find of making this word?

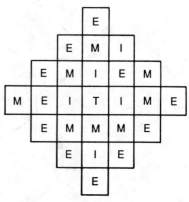

Fig. 2.26

9. Start at the bottom left-hand corner, R, on Fig. 2.27, and finish at the top right-hand corner, S, by only moving either upwards or to the right. On the way, moving from square to square, collect the word RABBITS.

    How many different ways are there of making this word?

B	I	T	S
B	B	I	T
A	B	B	I
R	A	B	B

Fig. 2.27

10. In each diagram of Fig. 2.28 a squirrel is hiding in one of the trees. The lines, with arrows, indicate the route the squirrel took on its daily journey. It travelled only once along each of the indicated paths between the trees. Find the tree it started from and the tree in which it is now hiding, and indicate on drawings, by numbering the various paths between the trees, those routes it may have followed from start to finish. How many different possible routes are there for each diagram?

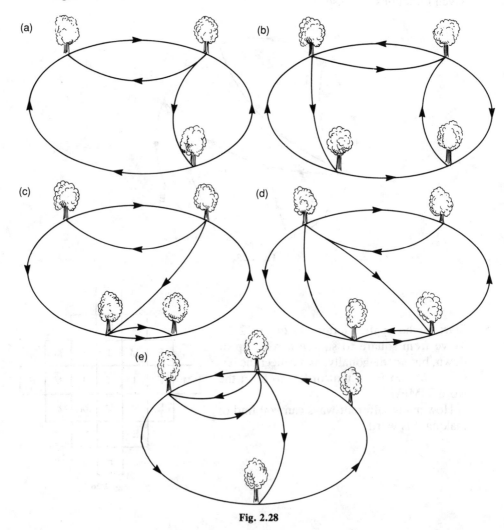

Fig. 2.28

COMMENTS

With many of the questions in this section the answers may be found more effectively if specially prepared solution sheets are available. These would exhibit the given diagram, enough times, for a different route to be coloured on each one. Displaying the routes helps one to consider new possibilities to be pursued as well as recording those routes already found.

Example 1

Suppose A, B, C and D are connected by roads as shown in Fig. 2.29. How many different ways are there from A to D if no road is used more than once in the same journey?

The solution may be assisted if numbers are jotted alongside the roads which indicate the number of ways of getting to that place from the start as shown in Fig. 2.30. Talk about, and discuss, how these numbers are obtained and what they signify. Altogether there are 24 ways from A to D.

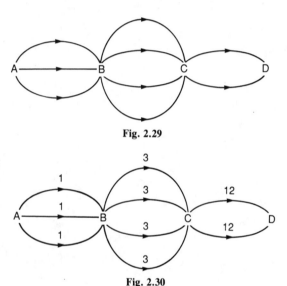

Fig. 2.29

Fig. 2.30

Example 2

How many different ways can the word HOLIDAY be read from left to right in Fig. 2.31, if each letter connects with its neighbour along one of the given lines?

These ways could be illustrated on a special recording sheet, with each diagram showing a different way of forming HOLI-DAY. This type of problem may also be linked with the number of ways along the paths of a suitably chosen network. Put numbers near the roads as shown in Fig. 2.32 to show the number of ways of

Fig. 2.31

getting there from H. Continue to insert numbers and see whether there are 20 ways of reading the word HOLIDAY.

These two examples, and comments, may assist with the solutions of some of the included problems.

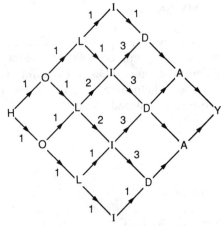

Fig. 2.32

S5 *Concerning Area*

(ANSWERS PAGES 166–7)

INVESTIGATIONS

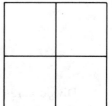

Fig. 2.33

1. Colour in half the square shown in Fig. 2.33, in different ways, using only the given lines as boundaries.

Fig. 2.34

2. Using the small squares only, in how many different ways can you colour in one half of the rectangle shown in Fig. 2.34?

Fig. 2.35

3. Find 6 different ways of cutting the square, shown in Fig. 2.35, along the lines, into two identical halves.

   Also find other ways of cutting the square, along the lines, into two parts of equal area which are not identical.

   Ensure there are no answers repeated involving rotations or flip-overs of previous answers.

4. Draw on centimetre squared paper, keeping to the lines, as many different shapes as you can with an area of 6 sq.cm. Which shape can you draw with the greatest number of sides?

5. Draw, on centimetre dot-lattice paper, various shapes each having an area of 3 sq.cm. Each shape must have a dot in each corner. Ensure there are no repeats entailing flip-overs or rotations.

6. Join any of the dots in a 3 by 3 dot-lattice (Fig. 2.36) to make shapes with an area of 3 squares. Each shape must have a dot in each corner and no lines must cross. Rotations and flip-overs are considered to produce the same shape. How many different shapes can you find?

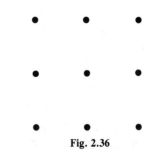

Fig. 2.36

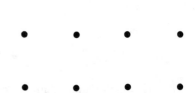

7. Divide a 12-dot lattice (Fig. 2.37) into two parts of equal area by joining dots with straight lines. Can you find 8 different ways? Ensure there are no repeats involving rotations and reflections.

Fig. 2.37

8. Make 12 different shapes within a 12-dot lattice (Fig. 2.37) each with an area of 5 squares. A dot must be at each corner and no lines must cross. Rotations and flip-overs are considered to make the same shape.

9. Can you find 5 different ways of dividing the 12-dot rectangular lattice of Fig. 2.37 into three parts of equal area by joining dots with straight lines. Ensure there are no flip-overs or rotations which produce the same shape.

10. How many different shapes of area 2 squares can you draw within a 3 by 3 dot-lattice as shown in Fig. 2.36? Rotations and flip-overs are considered to make the same shape. No lines may cross and every shape must have a dot in each corner.

11. Divide the 16-dot square of Fig. 2.38 into two parts of equal area by joining dots with straight lines. How many different ways can you find? Flip-overs and rotations are considered to make the same shape.

Fig. 2.38

12. Divide the square of Fig. 2.38 into three parts of equal area by joining dots with straight lines. Ensure there are no repeats, e.g. flip-overs and rotations. How many different ways can you find?

13. On centimetre square dotty paper draw squares with areas of 4, 9, 5, 8 and 10 sq.cm. All corners of each square must contain a dot.

14. On centimetre square dotty paper find as many different squares as possible which can be drawn with an area of 40 sq.cm or less.

15. Use centimetre square dotty paper. On it draw shapes with 3, 4, 5, ..., 11 and 12 straight sides, each having an area of 8 sq.cm. What shape can you draw with an area of 8 sq.cm which has the greatest number of sides?

COMMENTS

When drawing shapes of given area on squared paper discuss with the pupils various ways of making areas of ½, 1 and 1½ units. These basic shapes shown in Fig. 2.39 come in useful when building larger areas.

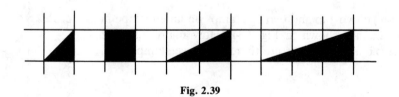

Fig. 2.39

To produce a shape with an area of 4½ squares, the joining together of shapes with areas 3 + ½ + ½ + ½, 3 + 1½, 3 + 1 + ½, 2 + 2 + ½, all need exploring.

S6 *Arrangements with Stamps*

(ANSWERS PAGE 167)

FOR INVESTIGATION

1. Arrange four 4p and one 2p stamp of an envelope in the manner shown in Fig. 2.40. How many different possible arrangements are there for these stamps?

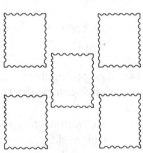

Fig. 2.40

2. How many different ways are there of sticking two 10p and two 2p stamps, side by side, in a row on an envelope?

3. Arrange two 10p and two 2p stamps on an envelope in the manner shown in Fig. 2.41. How many different possible arrangements are there for these stamps?

Fig. 2.41

4. Can you find 12 different ways of sticking one 10p, one 4p and two 2p stamps in a row on an envelope?

5. Arrange one 6p, one 2p and two 5p stamps on an envelope in the pattern shown in Fig. 2.41. How many different arrangements are there for these stamps?

6. Arrange one 6p, one 2p and three 5p stamps on an envelope in the pattern shown in Fig. 2.40. How many different possible arrangements are there for these stamps?

7. Three 2p and two 6p stamps are stuck, side by side, in a row on an envelope. How many different possible arrangements are there?

8. Arrange four 24p and two 10p stamps on a parcel in the pattern indicated in Fig. 2.42. How many possible arrangements are there for these stamps?

Fig. 2.42

9. One 6p, one 3p and three 5p stamps are stuck, side by side, in a row on an envelope. How many different possible arrangements are there?

10. How many different ways are there of sticking one 2p, two 5p and two 3p stamps in a row, side by side, on an envelope?

COMMENTS

When finding different arrangements of stamps the use of squared paper is invaluable because a square can represent a stamp. Squares may be drawn over quickly, and labelled or coloured in, when exploring and recording positional changes of particular stamps. Having a picture of what has already been done enables the pupil to realize those other possibilities which need consideration.

The following suggestions may prove helpful when answering the given questions.

Question 1

Let the 2p stamp, then a 4p stamp, occupy the central position.

Question 2

Put the two 10p stamps next to each other, then with one stamp and two stamps between them.

Question 3

Put the 10p stamps next to each other and then place them diagonally.

Question 4

Put the two 2p stamps next to each other, then with one stamp and two stamps between them.

Question 5

Put the 5p stamps next to each other and then place them diagonally.

Question 6

Let the 6p stamp, then the 2p stamp, then a 5p stamp occupy the central position.

Question 7

Put the two 6p stamps next to each other, then with one stamp, two stamps and three stamps between them.

Question 8

Put one 24p stamp, two 24p stamps, three 24p stamps in the top row.

Question 9

Put the 6p and 3p stamps next to each other, then with one, two and three 5p stamps between them.

Question 10

Put the two 5p stamps next to each other, then with one, two and three stamps between them.

S7 *Fitting Together Squares and Oblongs, Mainly*

(ANSWERS PAGES 167–8)

INVESTIGATIONS

1. Three ordinary first-class stamps are bought from the Post Office. The sales person tears these stamps, all joined together, from a sheet of stamps. How many different arrangements of these stamps are possible? Draw these arrangements on specially ruled rectangular grid paper.

2. How many different arrangements are possible for 4 attached stamps torn from a sheet of stamps by the Post Office sales person? Draw these possible ways on specially prepared rectangular grid paper.

3. Should 4 first-class stamps be purchased from the Post Office, the sales person could give the stamps either separately, or joined, or a combination of both. How many different possible ways are there for the presentation of these 4 stamps?

4. Use centimetre squared paper. How many different ways are there of joining four 1-centimetre squares with their sides coincident and touching? Draw these ways. Ensure there are no rotations or reflections which produce the same shape.

5. Use centimetre squared paper. Draw different ways of joining five 1-centimetre squares with their sides coincident and touching. Ensure there are no rotations or reflections which produce the same shape.

6. Use Multilink cubes. Join 2, then 3, then 4 and then 5 cubes in as many different ways as possible. In each case, all the cubes must touch the table top. Draw on centimetre triangular-dot paper the different shapes obtained in each case.

7.   Obtain centimetre squared paper. Three squares can be joined, corner to corner, in only two different ways as shown in Fig. 2.43. (Rotations and reflections are considered to produce the same shape.) How many different ways can four squares be joined, corner to corner, only?

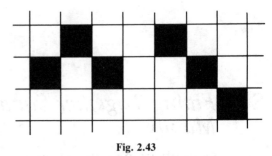

Fig. 2.43

Draw these ways keeping to the lines on the paper. How many different ways for joining 5 squares instead?

COMMENTS

A specially prepared rectangular grid is necessary when answering stamp arrangement questions. Squared paper, in this case, can cause confusion because stamps are not square, and two joined stamps produce two different configurations. Add one stamp to the arrangements of two stamps to obtain the different configurations for three stamps. Then add one stamp to the arrangements of three stamps to find different arrangements for four stamps. Similar principles apply to those activities involving the joining of squares or Multilink cubes. Naturally, the joining together of squares would be illustrated on squared paper.

S8 Making Shapes by Fitting Together Paper Triangles and Rectangles

(ANSWERS PAGE 168)

ACTIVITIES

1. Make a cardboard right-angled triangular template, as shown in Fig. 2.44, with sides adjacent to the right angle 5 cm long. Draw around it and cut out 15 paper triangles. Use only three of these triangles, at a time, and put them side by side on the table with only equal sides touching to make a shape.

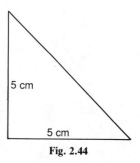

Fig. 2.44

   How many different shapes can be made? Stick them on paper to make a display. Ensure there are no repeats made by the rotation or reflection of a shape made previously.

2. On centimetre squared paper draw and cut out 1 square and 2 triangles to the sizes shown in Fig. 2.45. (Cardboard templates could be made instead to the given dimensions and then drawn around.) Put these three shapes together, on the table, side by side, with equal sides coinciding to make a new shape. Repeat this and make other different shapes and stick them on paper to form a display. Ensure there are no repeats, e.g. rotations and reflections.

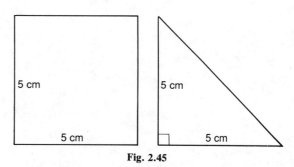

Fig. 2.45

3. On centimetre squared paper cut out 1 rectangle and 2 triangles to the dimensions given in Fig. 2.46. (The length of the rectangle and the longest side of the triangle are the same: approximately 7.1 cm.) Put these three shapes together, side by side on the table, with only equal sides touching, to make a new shape. Repeat this and make other shapes and stick them on paper to make a display. Ensure there are no repeats, e.g. rotations and reflections.

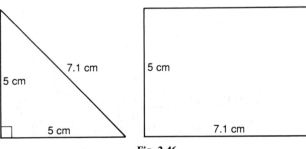

Fig. 2.46

S9 Folding Paper Shapes

(ANSWERS PAGE 168)

ACTIVITIES

1. Draw around a plastic or cardboard rectangle, about 8 cm long and 4 cm wide, and cut out rectangular pieces of paper of the same size. Fold a rectangle once and stick the two parts together. How many sides has this new shape? Repeat the procedure with other rectangles and make as many shapes as possible with different numbers of sides. Display these shapes on a wall chart. Near each shape write its number of sides and possibly its name, e.g. 9 sides – nonagon.

    Repeat this activity using instead

    (a) equilateral triangles of side approximately 6 cm,
    (b) squares of side roughly 8 cm, and
    (c) regular hexagons of side 2–3 cm, or more.

2. Cut out rectangular pieces of paper of the same size by drawing around a plastic or cardboard rectangle about 8 cm long and 5 cm wide. Fold a rectangle once and open it out. Colour each part of the rectangle a different colour and count the number of sides in each part and record them. The division shown in

    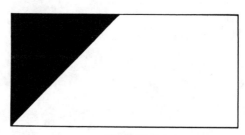

    Fig. 2.47

    Fig. 2.47, which creates a triangle and a quadrilateral, could be recorded as (3,4). How many different divisions can you find? Display them.

    This activity could be repeated using congruent

    (a) triangles
    (b) regular pentagons
    (c) regular hexagons, or
    (d) regular octagons.

3. Cut out paper equilateral triangles of the same size by drawing around a plastic or cardboard template of side approximately 8 cm. Fold a triangle and open it out. Fold it again and open it out. Line in the folds and colour each part of the triangle a different colour. Count the number of sides in each part and record them. The division shown in Fig. 2.48 could be recorded as $(3, 3, 4, 4)$. How. many different ways can you find for dividing a triangle using two folds? Display the results on a wall chart.

Fig. 2.48

The procedure described could also be followed using

(a) rectangles
(b) regular pentagons
(c) regular hexagons, or
(d) regular octagons.

S10 *Drawing Lines and Joining Dots*

(ANSWERS PAGE 169)

FOR INVESTIGATION

1. Various ways of joining 4 dots, placed in different positions, are illustrated in Fig. 2.49. The least number of lines needed is 3 and the greatest number is 6. They may also be joined with 5 lines.

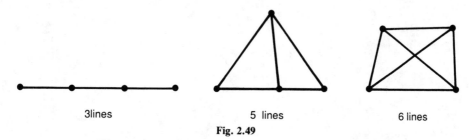

3 lines   5 lines   6 lines

Fig. 2.49

Investigate, in a similar manner, the number of straight lines needed to join 5 dots, then 6 dots and 7 dots, if each dot is joined, where possible, to each of the others. In each case display the results, stating the greatest and least number of lines required and other possible numbers of lines between these values.

2. Different ways of dividing up a circle using 3 straight lines are shown in Fig. 2.50. The least number of parts is four and the greatest number seven. Altogether it can be divided into 4, 5, 6 or 7 parts.

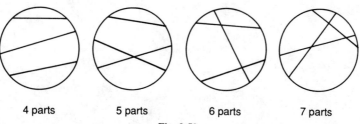

4 parts   5 parts   6 parts   7 parts

Fig. 2.50

Investigate, in a similar manner, the number of parts a circle can be divided into with 4, then 5 and 6 straight lines. In each case, display the results, and state the least and greatest number of parts and other possible numbers obtainable.

3. If 2 dots on the circumference of a circle are joined with a straight line the circle is divided into 2 parts. Three dots on the circumference will, when *all* are joined, divide a circle into 4 parts, as shown in Fig. 2.51.

How many parts will a circle be divided into if 4 dots on its circumference are all joined to each of the others? What about 5 dots? Enter these results in a table as shown in Fig. 2.52. Use these data to predict the number of parts a circle will be divided into when 6, then 7, dots are joined. Draw large circles to check these answers. Were your predictions correct?

Fig. 2.51

Number of dots	2	3	4	5	6	7
Number of parts	2	4				

Fig. 2.52

Puzzlers

P1 *Where Are They?*

(ANSWERS PAGE 173)

FOR SOLUTION

1. A green counter, a black counter and a white counter are put in a row on the table. The white counter is to the left of the green one. The green counter is to the right of the black counter and next to it. Draw the three counters and colour them in.

2. An orange counter, a blue counter and a red counter are placed in a row on the table. The red counter is to the left of the orange counter. The blue counter is not next to the orange counter. Draw and colour in these counters.

3. Four stamps are placed side by side in a row. Their colours are red, green, blue and orange. The orange stamp is not at the end of the row. The red stamp is between the green stamp and the blue stamp but not next to the green stamp. The blue stamp is to the left of the orange one. Draw the row of stamps and colour them in.

4. Four houses in a row are coloured white, cream, green and brown. The green house is not at the end of the row and is not next to the brown house. The white house is next to the green house but not next to the brown one. The cream house is to the left of the green house. Draw the houses and colour them in.

5. Four children called Peter, Brian, Yvonne and Gemma stand side by side facing you in a row. The girls are next to each other but the boys are not. Peter stands on Gemma's left. Brian does not stand next to Gemma. Put names beside the children in a diagram.

6. Five coins, a penny, a twopence, a fivepence, a tenpence and a twentypence, are put in a row on the table. The highest value coin is in the middle. The fivepence is on the left of the twentypence but not next to it. The twopence and the fivepence

are separated by two other coins. The penny is not at the end of the row. Draw five circles to represent these coins and write a value on each one.

COMMENTS

Either prepare some coloured cardboard discs and move them about on the table according to the instructions given in the question, or put arrow diagrams on paper, singly at first, according to the information given, then combine them into one system.

Example

A red, a white and a green counter are placed in a row on the table. The white counter is to the left of the blue counter and to the right of the green counter. The red counter is left of the blue counter and not next to the green one. What are the colours of the counters from left to right?

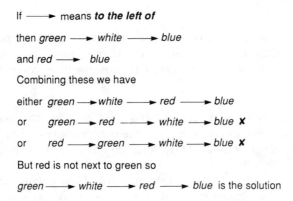

The counters are green, white, red and blue from left to right.

P2 *Name the Animals*

(ANSWERS PAGE 173)

FOR SOLUTION

1. A horse and a cow are called Tulip and Princess. The horse is not called Tulip. What animal is Princess?

2. Jean, Richard and Katherine each have a pet. The pets are a rabbit, a mouse and a guinea-pig. Jean's pet has no tail. Katherine's pet has a fluffy tail. Which pet does each child have?

3. Patch, Ginger and Champion are the names of a cat, a horse and a dog. Champion loves to eat grass. Ginger is the smallest animal. What is the dog's name? Which animal is Ginger?

4. A pig, a horse and a camel are called Gertie, Omar and Duke. Gertie lives in a sty. The camel is not called Duke. What is each animal's name?

5. Patch, Garth and Winnie are the names of a horse, a dog and a mouse. Patch is larger than Winnie. Winnie and Garth cannot bark. Name each animal.

6. Robert, Dora and Catherine each have a pet. They have a cat, a dog and a rabbit. No child has an animal which starts with the same letter as his or her name. Robert's pet can bark. Which pet is kept by each child?

7. Rebecca, Shabinah and David were asked to name their favourite zoo animal. The animals named were a sea-lion, an elephant and a giraffe. Shabinah's animal didn't have a long neck and David's animal didn't have a trunk. Rebecca's animal ate fish and could swim well. Name each child's favourite zoo animal.

8. Jason, Hector and Susie are the names of three pet animals: a large dog, a cat and a mouse. Susie is smaller than the cat. Jason is younger than the dog. What is each pet called?

9. A cat, a mouse, an Alsatian dog and a horse are called Noble, Prince, Tiny and Rosie. Prince and the cat like each other. Tiny is afraid of the horse. Prince, Rosie and the horse are the largest of the four animals. What is the name of the cat?

COMMENTS

Example

Ali, Roy and Dawn each have a pet. They have a hamster, a dog and a budgerigar. Dawn's pet has feathers. Ali does not have a dog. Which pet belongs to each child?

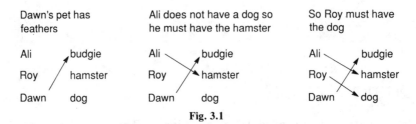

Fig. 3.1

Either use arrow diagrams (Fig. 3.1) to connect names with pets as the information is read through, or use labelled grids (Fig. 3.2), either three by three, or four by four.

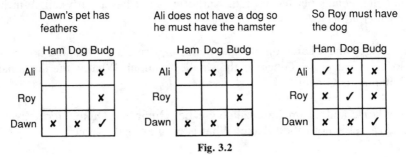

Fig. 3.2

Ali has a hamster, Dawn a budgerigar and Roy a dog.

P3 *Family Matters*

(ANSWERS PAGE 173)

FOR SOLUTION

1. Ruth, Diane, Paul and William belong to two different families. William is Ruth's only brother. Ruth and Diane are not sisters. Which children are in each family?

2. Karen, Eleanor, Nicholas and Graham belong to two different families. Eleanor is not the sister of Nicholas or Karen. Graham is not Nicholas's brother. Which children are in each family?

3. Julie, Yvette, Andy and Nathan are two sets of twins aged 10 and 4. Julie is much younger than Andy. Yvette is much older than Nathan. Which twins are aged 4?

COMMENTS

Write each child's name on a piece of paper and then move these four names about on the table top, according to the information given, until a successful grouping is found.

P4 *Putting Things in Order*

(ANSWERS PAGE 174)

FOR CONSIDERATION

1. Michelle, Duane, Alison and Robert are four children. Michelle is taller than Alison. Robert is shorter than Duane but taller than Michelle. Which child is the shortest? Which child is the tallest?

2. Glenn, Eddie and Susan are aged 14, 12 and 9. Glenn is younger than Susan but older than Eddie. How old is each child?

3. Sîan, Steve, Greg and Natalie have ages of 12, 10, 9 and 7. Greg is younger than Natalie but older than Sîan. Natalie is younger than Steve. How old is each child?

4. Stella, Matthew, Bill and Janet have ages of 8, 10, 12 and 14. Matthew and Stella are both younger than Bill. The oldest child is a girl and the youngest is a boy. What is each child's age?

5. Ken, Robert, Osman and Gary play in a hockey team. Last season they scored 8, 12, 20 and 24 goals. Robert scored fewer goals than Ken but more goals than Gary. Osman scored more goals than Gary but fewer than Robert. How many goals did Ken, Robert, Osman and Gary each score?

COMMENTS

Use arrow diagrams to connect first names, the arrows meaning 'is heavier than', 'is younger than', 'scored more goals than', and so on. Use a relationship diagram for each piece of information and then slot them together to make one diagram. Numbers, where appropriate, can then be assigned to these names.

Example

Duane, Osman, Barry and Nathan are four children. Nathan is heavier than Barry but lighter than Osman. Duane is not the heaviest but is heavier than Nathan. Arrange the children in order of weight, heaviest to lightest.

If ⟶ means *is heavier than*

Osman ⟶ Nathan ⟶ Barry and Duane ⟶ Nathan

Combining these we obtain

either Duane ⟶ Osman ⟶ Nathan ⟶ Barry

or Osman ⟶ Duane ⟶ Nathan ⟶ Barry

Duane is not the heaviest so

Osman ⟶ Duane ⟶ Nathan ⟶ Barry

From heaviest to lightest the children are Osman, Duane, Nathan and Barry.

P5   *What's What?*

(ANSWERS PAGES 174–5)

FOR SOLUTION

1.   Mr Adams, Mrs Hill and Mrs Young each have a car. One car is red, one is blue and the other is green. Mrs Young's car is not red. Of the three colours, Mrs Hill's car colour has the most letters in it. What colour is each person's car?

2.   Betty, Lizzie and Fatima each bought one item at the shop. They bought a can of lemonade, a bar of chocolate and an ice-cream. Before going to the shop Lizzie said the weather was too cold to buy ice-cream. Betty said she felt hungry but not thirsty. Fatima said she was not going to buy lemonade. What did each person buy?

3.   Mrs Smith, Mr Baker and Mrs Green went to the fruit shop and each bought only one kind of fruit. Altogether they bought bananas, apples and grapes. The fruit Mr Baker bought was not yellow and it did not have a core. Mrs Smith's fruit was not nearly round. What kind of fruit did each person buy?

4.   Debbie bought 3 bowls of crocuses. One bowl was white, another was green and the other was brown. The crocuses were yellow, blue and white, and each bowl contained only one colour of crocus. Each bowl contained crocuses a different colour than the bowl. The yellow crocuses were not in the white bowl and the white crocuses were not in the brown bowl. What colour of crocus was in each bowl?

5.   Mr Ahmed, Mr Wilson and Mrs Hall each have a car. One car is blue, one is grey and the other is brown. Mr Ahmed's car is not brown. Mr Wilson's car is not grey or brown. What colour is each person's car?

6.   A pilot, a chef and a sailor are named Grey, White and Black. Grey and Black do not know much about cooking. Grey cannot swim and easily gets seasick. Name the chef and the pilot.

7. Three children have first names of James, Diana and Edward and their surnames are Davis, Jones and Evans. No child has a surname and first name starting with the same letter. Evans is not a girl. What are the full names of the children?

8. Mrs Brown, Mrs Scott and Mrs Cook each have a daughter. The girls are called Tracey, June and Mary. June is not called Brown. Tracey is not called Scott. Mary is not called Cook. Cook is older than June. What are the girls' full names?

9. Alice, Marie and George have surnames of Black, Farmer and Price. George's last name is not Farmer. Alice's surname is not Price. Marie's last name is not Black. Alice is taller than Black. What are the children's names?

10. Don, Lizzie and Jill have surnames of Allen, Clark and Roberts. Allen and Jill are friends. Lizzie is taller than Roberts but shorter than Clark. Don lives near Roberts. What are the full names of the people?

11. Derek, Jessica and Sophie have surnames of Wood, Taylor and Russell. Wood and Sophie often go shopping together. Jessica is taller than Taylor but shorter than Russell. Derek lives near Taylor. What are the full names of the people?

12. Gerald, Henry and Keith have surnames of Watts, Atkins and Carter. Watts is taller than Henry. Keith and Carter are friends. Gerald is older than Watts. Henry's surname is not Atkins. What are the full names of the people?

13. Anne, Ben, Catherine and Dennis have surnames of Adams, Baker, Cook and Davis. No person's first name and surname start with the same letter. Ben is taller than Cook. Anne is older than Davis. Ben is not called Davis. Catherine is not called Baker. Anne is not called Cook. What is each person's full name?

14. Carol, Sharon and Lucy each have one pencil. One pencil is red, one is black and the other is blue. The red pencil does not belong to Sharon and the blue pencil does not belong to Carol. Sharon's pencil is longer than Carol's pencil. The black pencil and the blue pencil are both shorter than Lucy's pencil. What is the colour of each child's pencil, and which pencil is longest and which is shortest?

15. Lucille, Claire and Rhiannon are three girls. One wears a white blouse, another a pink blouse and the other a green blouse. One wears a blue skirt, another a grey skirt and the third a brown skirt. Lucille does not wear the grey skirt or green blouse. Rhiannon does not wear the white blouse or blue skirt. Claire wears the green blouse but not a grey skirt. The white blouse is worn with the blue skirt. Who wears which clothes?

16. Sally, Charlotte and Lynda are friends. One has fair hair, one has brown hair and the other has black hair. One wears a grey skirt, another a green and the other a navy blue skirt. Charlotte does not wear a grey skirt and does not have black hair. Sally does not have fair hair and does not wear a green skirt. The brown-haired girl does not wear a navy blue skirt. The girl with fair hair wears a grey skirt. Who wears what and what colour is her hair?

COMMENTS

Write names, colours or other necessary words on separate pieces of paper which may then be moved about on the table top according to the information given.

Alternatively use arrow diagrams as in Fig. 3.3 or use labelled three by three, or four by four, square grids as in Fig. 3.4.

Example

Ann, Mick and Liza each have a car. One has a white car, one a blue car and the other a grey car. Ann's car is not white. The blue car does not belong to Ann or Liza. What colour is each person's car?

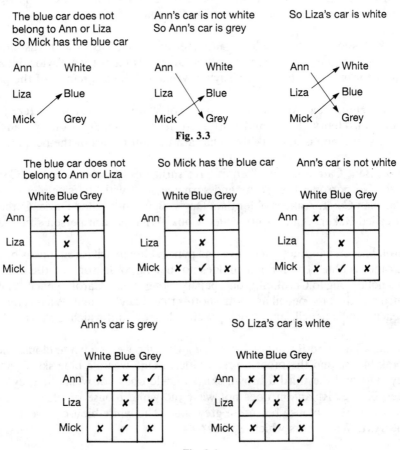

Fig. 3.3

Fig. 3.4

Ann has a grey car, Mick a blue car and Liza a white car.

P6 *Measuring Out Liquid*

(ANSWERS PAGE 175)

FOR SOLUTION

1. A 3-litre measure and a 5-litre measure are available and plenty of water. How could these be used to obtain 1 litre of water?

2. How could 1 litre of water be measured out using only an 8-litre measure, a 3-litre measure, and plenty of water?

3. Gareth has only a 2-litre container and a 5-litre container. How could he use them to measure out 1 litre of water? Could 3 litres also be measured out?

4. Soraya has only a 4-litre container and a 3-litre container. How could these be used to measure out 2 litres of water? What about measuring out 1 litre?

5. A 5-litre and an 8-litre container are available, and water. Explain how these could be used to measure out 1 litre. What other amounts, in whole litres, between 1 litre and 8 litres, could also be measured out?

COMMENTS

Consider these approaches.

(a) Pour as much of the contents of the smaller measure, filled twice or more, into the larger to fill it, perhaps more than once. How much remains in the smaller measure?

(b) Pour as much of the contents of the larger measure, filled possibly more than once, into the smaller vessel to fill it, perhaps more than once. How much is left in the larger measure?

Example

Should the measures available be a 4-litre and a 7-litre, then 1 litre could be measured out by filling the 4-litre measure twice and pouring into the 7-litre vessel. Two litres could be measured out by filling the 7-litre measure twice and pouring into the 4-litre measure to fill it three times.

P7 *Crossing the River*

(ANSWER PAGE 175)

FOR SOLUTION

Two men and two boys all need to cross a river. They have a rowing-boat which carries only 1 man or 2 boys at a time. All four can row a boat. Explain how they can arrange themselves in order to cross in the boat.

COMMENTS

Use plastic People Sorts, and a box lid, to act out the crossing, recording or remembering the stages involved.

P8 *Find the Heaviest*

(ANSWERS PAGES 175–6)

TO BE SOLVED

1. There are 9 large glass marbles of the same size and colour. One of these marbles is heavier than the other 8 marbles, which weigh the same. Find this heavier marble in just *two* balancings using a sensitive common balance.

2. There are 27 gold coins of the same size and colour. Twenty-six of them are the same weight whilst one coin is a heavier forgery, being made of denser metal and then thinly gold plated. Find this forged coin in just *three* balancings using a sensitive common balance.

COMMENT

Use a common balance and the given number of marbles (coins), together with one larger heavier marble (coin), and manipulate them to find the heaviest marble (coin). The actions with the balance help to clarify the reasoning involved.

P9 *Find the Number*

(ANSWERS PAGE 176)

ACTIVITY

A person thinks of a whole number less than 50. Another child, or children, asks that person questions to which he or she may answer only 'yes' or 'no', in order to find out what that number is. What is the least number of questions to be asked in order to identify, on every occasion, the number thought of?

What would be the least number of questions if, instead, the number chosen is less than 100? Suppose it were less than 200?

COMMENTS

Halve the range with each of the questions asked to minimize the number of questions. Suppose the number was 23. Ask,

Is it 25 or more? No	(It is a number from 1 to 24 inclusive within 1–12 or 13–24)
Is it 12 or less? No	(It is a number from 13 to 24 inclusive within 13–18 or 19–24)
Is it 19 or more? Yes	(It is a number from 19 to 24 inclusive within 19–21 or 22–24)
Is it 22 or more? Yes	(It is 22, 23 or 24)
Is it 23 or less? Yes	(It is 22 or 23)
Is it 22? No	(It is 23)

So the number was 23 and six questions were asked. Suppose instead the number thought of was 36. Ask,

Is it 25 or more? Yes	(It is a number from 25 to 49 inclusive within 25–37 or 38–49)
Is it 38 or more? No	(It is a number from 25 to 37 inclusive within 25–31 or 32–37)
Is it 31 or less? No	(It is a number from 32 to 37 inclusive within 32–34 or 35–37)
Is it 34 or less? No	(It is 35, 36 or 37)
Is it 36 or more? Yes	(It is 36 or 37)
Is it 36? Yes	

So the number was 36 and six questions were asked.

Six carefully worded questions using the mid-value of the range will locate any number, less than 50, if the above procedure is used. For numbers less than 100, another commencing question is needed, such as, 'Is it 50 or more?'. For numbers less than 200, an additional starting question, 'Is it 100 or more?' needs to be asked.

Allow time between questions for pupils to jot down the new range of possible numbers as each question is asked. A tape-recording of the proceedings is extremely useful because the questions asked, and ways of decreasing their number, can be discussed later.

P10 *Who's 'It'?*

(ANSWERS PAGE 176)

FOR CONSIDERATION

Six children, Adrian, Laura, Simone, Christine, Phil and Carl, standing in that order, clockwise, in an approximate circle, use the six words of the sentence 'Humpty Dumpty sat on a wall' to find who is to be 'it'. They repeat the sentence and every person 'counted' with the sixth word (wall) around the circle, clockwise, is eliminated each time, until only one person remains. Check that, should the first word of the sentence start with Laura, then Phil would be 'it'. Suppose Adrian was 'it'; with which person did the sentence start?

Repeat the procedure using instead the five-word phrase 'One, two, buckle my shoe', and starting with Laura find who would be 'it'. Suppose Christine was 'it'; from where did the count start?

Again, supposing the sentence used was 'Jack and Jill went up the hill', and Phil was 'it', from which person did the sentence start?

COMMENTS

Write the six children's names, roughly in a circle, start with one of them and using the sentence find who would be 'it'. Knowing the start person and 'it', and their relative positions, enables future 'it's to be predicted without repeating the sentence.

P11   *Free Offers*

(ANSWERS PAGE 176)

FOR SOLUTION

1. A manufacturer offers a coupon for a free 100 g jar of coffee for every four 100 g coffee labels collected and presented. If 28 jars of coffee were bought initially, how many free 100 g jars of coffee could be obtained?

2. A manufacturer supplies a voucher for a free 125 g bar of soap for every three 125 g soap wrappers presented. What is the least number of bars of soap to be purchased in order to obtain 4 free bars?

3. A manufacturer offers a free packet of jelly for every 2 jelly packet fronts, of the same brand, submitted to them. How many packets of jelly need to be purchased to obtain 7 free packets altogether?

COMMENTS

Do not forget that free jars have labels. Use a starting number and note the number of free items it produces, and then increase or decrease it accordingly until the required number of free items is obtained.

P12 *Numbers for Letters*

(ANSWERS PAGES 176–7)

TO BE SOLVED

1. If cat ⟶ 3
   and elephant ⟶ 8
   and hippopotamus ⟶ 12
   then chimpanzee ⟶ ?

2. If daffodil ⟶ 4
   and crocus ⟶ 3
   and foxglove ⟶ 6
   and marigold ⟶ 13
   then rose ⟶ ?

3. If car ⟶ 22
   and boat ⟶ 38
   and bus ⟶ 42
   then bicycle ⟶ ?

4. If elephant ⟶ 15
   and bear ⟶ 4
   and monkey ⟶ 8
   and cheetah ⟶ 12
   then jaguar ⟶ ?

5. If chestnut ⟶ 4
   and beech ⟶ 1
   and elm ⟶ 1
   and sycamore ⟶ 2
   then larch ⟶ ?

6. If chicken ⟶ 9
   and pig ⟶ 4
   and goat ⟶ 6
   and sheep ⟶ 7
   then goose ⟶ ?

COMMENTS

Consider these ideas. Are the words and numbers related to:

(a) $a = 1$, $b = 2$, $c = 3$, ..., $z = 26$, and then addition or some other operation; or
(b) the lengths of the words; or
(c) the starting letters of the words and their alphabetical positions; or
(d) the number of vowels or consonants; or
(e) some operation between the number of vowels and consonants, such as multiplication or subtraction?

P13 *Missing Links*

(ANSWERS PAGE 177)

FOR SOLUTION

In the following questions what numbers should replace the question marks?

1. If   7   3   1 ——→9
   and   5   9   3 ——→11
   and   8   9   4 ——→13
   then   6   8   5 ——→?

4. If   2 * 5 ——→6
   and   4 * 7 ——→24
   and   5 * 6 ——→26
   then   3 * 8 ——→?

2. If   7   2   4 ——→20
   and   6   3   5 ——→15
   and   9   3   3 ——→18
   then   8   1   4 ——→?

5. If   2 * 4 ——→16
   and   1 * 6 ——→12
   and   4 * 3 ——→24
   then   2 * 5 ——→?

3. If   14   7   3 ——→5
   and   16   4   2 ——→6
   and   18   3   1 ——→7
   then   10   2   3 ——→?

COMMENTS

Consider the insertion of arithmetical signs between the numbers or the translation of * into arithmetical procedures.

P14 *Inconsecutive Numbers*

(ANSWERS PAGES 177–8)

FOR SOLUTION

1. Put the numbers 2, 3, 4, 5 and 6 on Fig. 3.5, one number per circle, such that the two numbers at the ends of each connecting line do not differ by 1.

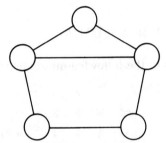

Fig. 3.5

2. Put the numbers 1, 2, 3, 4, 5 and 6 on Fig. 3.6, one number per circle, such that the two numbers at the ends of each connecting line are not consecutive.

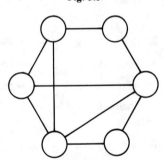

Fig. 3.6

3. Put the numbers 1, 2, 3, 4, 5 and 6 on Fig. 3.7, one number per circle, such that the two numbers at the ends of each connecting line are not consecutive.

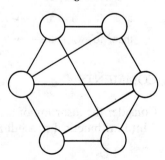

Fig. 3.7

4. Put the numbers 1,2,3,4,5 and 6 on Fig. 3.8, one number in each circle, such that the numbers at the ends of each connecting line do not differ by 1. How many solutions can you find?

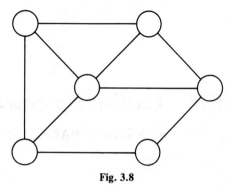

Fig. 3.8

COMMENTS

Find a circle with most connecting lines going to it. Put each number, in turn, into this circle and consider where the remaining numbers may fit.

P15 *Cutting Up Squares*

(ANSWERS PAGES 178–9)

FOR INVESTIGATION

1. Cut the square shown in Fig. 3.9, along the lines, into four parts so that each part has four different letters on it.

A	C	C	B
B	B	D	A
D	A	D	B
D	C	C	A

Fig. 3.9

2. Cut the square shown in Fig. 3.10 along the lines into five parts so that each part has all the letters of the word LEMON on it.

L	M	M	O	L
O	N	N	E	L
O	E	N	O	E
N	M	M	M	O
L	E	E	N	L

Fig. 3.10

Q	A	U	U	U	S
Q	R	S	S	A	A
A	E	S	Q	R	R
U	E	R	S	E	Q
U	R	R	U	A	E
E	A	S	Q	Q	E

Fig. 3.11

3. The square in Fig. 3.11 contains the letters of the word SQUARE, six times. Cut the square along the lines into six parts such that each part contains the letters of the word SQUARE.

COMMENTS

Some of the parts of the boundaries may be fitted in readily by finding adjacent squares containing the same letter. Talk with the pupils about the implication of this. Use squared paper when answering these questions.

P16 *Misprints*

(ANSWERS PAGE 179)

FOR CONSIDERATION

1. The numbers on the square in Fig. 3.12 have a particular property. One number, however, has been printed incorrectly. Find this number and correct it.

2	7	4	2
5	3	1	6
2	2	8	3
6	3	3	4

Fig. 3.12

2. One of the numbers in the square of Fig. 3.13 has been incorrectly printed. Which one may it be, if the numbers in rows and columns have something in common?

6	4	2	8
1	9	3	7
10	3	6	2
3	5	9	3

Fig. 3.13

3. Which number in the square of Fig. 3.14 has been incorrectly printed, if the numbers inserted should have a particular property?

16	4	9	1
2	5	11	13
8	7	6	9
4	14	5	7

Fig. 3.14

7	10	6	12	6	9
14	9	8	7	6	6
6	5	16	4	7	11
8	13	3	2	12	12
11	3	9	16	7	4
4	10	7	9	12	8

4. The numbers on the square of Fig. 3.15 have something in common. Correct the one number which, however, has been misprinted.

Fig. 3.15

P17   *Numbers for Symbols*

(ANSWERS PAGE 179)

FOR SOLUTION

1. What numbers in Fig. 3.16 should replace the question marks?

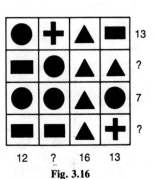

Fig. 3.16

2. What numbers in Fig. 3.17 should replace the question marks?

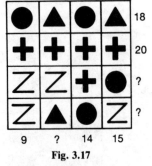

Fig. 3.17

3. What numbers in Fig. 3.18 do the question marks represent?

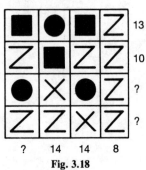

Fig. 3.18

COMMENTS

Find a row, or column, which contains only one kind of symbol, and find its value. This will generate another row, or column, which includes only one kind of missing symbol, so this may also be evaluated. Repeat this process until all four symbol values are found. The value of each question mark can then be ascertained.

P18 *Magic Squares*

(ANSWER PAGE 180)

FOR CONSIDERATION

The squares shown in Fig. 3.19 are 'magic'. What do you notice about the numbers on each square? Find out something also about the numbers in each row, each column and the diagonals. Why may these squares be called 'magic'?

30	39	48	1	10	19	28
38	47	7	9	18	27	29
46	6	8	17	26	35	37
5	14	16	25	34	36	45
13	15	24	33	42	44	4
21	23	32	41	43	3	12
22	31	40	49	2	11	20

17	24	1	8	15
23	5	7	14	16
4	6	13	20	22
10	12	19	21	3
11	18	25	2	9

8	1	6
3	5	7
4	9	2

Fig. 3.19

Inspect the numbers in the three magic squares of Fig. 3.19 extremely carefully. As a result, put numbers on the empty grid of Fig. 3.20 in order to make a 9 by 9 'magic' square.

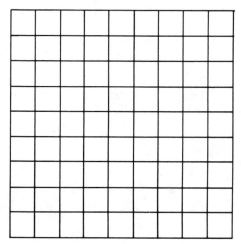

Fig. 3.20

Answers to Number Activities

N1 *SHARING LEMONADE AND BOTTLES* (page 3)

F = full bottle; HF = half-bottle; EB = empty bottle.

1. Two children each receive 2F, 1HF and 2EB, and the other receives 1F, 3HF and 1EB.

2. *Either* two children each receive 2F, 3HF and 2E, and the other receives 3F, 1HF and 3EB, *or* two children each receive 3F, 1HF and 3EB, and the other receives 1F, 5HF and 1EB.

3. (a) *Either* two children each receive 3F, 2HF and 3EB, and the other receives 2F, 4HF and 2EB; *or* two children each receive 2F, 4HF and 2EB, and the other receives 4F and 4EB; *or* two children each receive 4F and 4EB, and the other receives 8HF; *or* one child receives 4F and 4EB; another receives 3F, 2HF and 3EB, and another 1F, 6HF and 1EB.
    (b) *Either* two children each receive 2F and 2EB, and four children each receive 1F, 2HF and 1EB; *or* three children each receive 2F and 2EB, two children each receive 1F, 2HF and 1EB, and the other receives 4HF; *or* four children each receive 2F and 2EB, and two children each receive 4HF.

N2 *FINDING POSSIBLE, AND PARTICULAR, SCORES ON SPECIAL DARTBOARDS* (pages 4–5)

1. Least score: 3. Greatest score: 12.
    Possible scores: 3, 4, 5, 6, 7, 8, 9, 10, 11 and 12.
    Easiest scores to obtain are 6, 7, 8 and 9.
    Hardest scores to obtain are 3, 4, 11 and 12.

2. Possible scores are 6, 8, 10, 12, 14, 16 and 18.
    Greatest score: 18. Least score: 6.
    Ways of scoring 10 are (2, 2, 6) and (2, 4, 4).

3. Possible scores are 6, 7, 8, 9, 10, 11, 12, 13, 14 and 15.
    Three ways of scoring 9: (3, 3, 3), (2, 2, 5) and (2, 3, 4).
    Three ways of scoring 10: (3, 3, 4), (2, 4, 4) and (2, 3, 5).
    Three ways of scoring 11: (3, 3, 5), (3, 4, 4) and (2, 4, 5).
    Scores of 10 and 11 can each be obtained in three ways.

4. (a) 2 ways: (2, 3, 5, 10) and (2, 3, 6, 9).
    (b) 5 ways: (3, 5, 6, 6), (2, 5, 5, 8), (3, 3, 5, 9), (3, 3, 6, 8) and (2, 2, 6, 10).
    (c) 1 way: (2, 6, 6, 6).

5. 7 ways of scoring 45.
    (15, 15, 15) if darts score the same; (5, 20, 20), (10, 10, 25) and (5, 5, 35) if two darts score the same; (5, 10, 30), (10, 15, 20) and (5, 15, 25) if all darts score differently.

N3   *OBTAINING PARTICULAR SCORES ON A NORMAL DARTBOARD* (page 6)

1. Some possible scores are:

   (25, 20, 5) (25, 19, 6) (25, 18, 7) (25, 17, 8)
   (25, 16, 9) (25, 15, 10) (25, 14, 11) (25, 13, 12)
   (20, 19, 11) (20, 18, 12) (20, 17, 13) (20, 16, 14)
   (19, 18, 13) (19, 17, 14) (19, 16, 15) (18, 17, 15)

2. D = double. Some possible scores are:

   (D20, 11, 1) (D20, 10, 2) (D20, 9, 3) (D20, 8, 4)
   (D20, 7, 5) (D19, 13, 1) (D19, 12, 2) (D19, 11, 3)
   (D19, 10, 4) (D19, 9, 5) (D19, 8, 6) (D18, 15, 1)
   (D18, 14, 2) (D18, 13, 3) (D18, 12, 4) (D17, 16, 2)
   (D17, 15, 3)   (D17, 14, 4)

3. D = double; T = Treble. Some possible scores are:

   (T15, D5, 12) (T15, D4, 14) (T15, D3, 16) (T15, D2, 18)
   (T15, D1, 20) (T20, D3, 1) (T20, D2, 3) (T20, D1, 5)
   (T19, D1, 8) (T19, D2, 6) (T19, D3, 4) (T19, D4, 2)

N4   *FINDING POSSIBLE, AND PARTICULAR, SCORES AT A SHOOTING GALLERY* (page 7)

1. (a) Least score: 12. Greatest score: 42.
   (b) Five ways of scoring 32: (16, 14, 2), (16, 12, 4), (16, 10, 6), (14, 10, 8) and (14, 12, 6).
   (c) Four ways of scoring 16 or less: (6, 4, 2), (8, 4, 2), (8, 6, 2) and (10, 4, 2).
   (d) Four ways of scoring 38 or more: (16, 14, 12), (16, 14, 10), (16, 14, 8) and (16, 12, 10).

2. Eleven different ways of scoring 15 or more: (10, 6, 5), (10, 6, 4), (10, 6, 3), (10, 6, 2), (10, 5, 4), (10, 5, 3), (10, 5, 2), (10, 4, 3), (10, 4, 2), (10, 3, 2) and (6, 5, 4).

N5   *LENGTH* (page 8)

EE = end to end; AL = alongside each other.

1. 6 cm rod to measure out 6 cm; 6 cm and 8 cm EE to measure 14 cm; 6 cm and 9 cm EE to measure 15 cm; 8 cm and 9 cm EE to measure 17 cm; 8 cm and 6 cm AL to measure 2 cm; 9 cm and 6 cm AL to measure 3 cm.
   Other distances which can be measured are 1, 5, 7, 8, 9, 11 and 23 cm.

2. Putting rods, *only* end to end, distances which can be measured out are 11, 13, 14, 15, 16, 18, 19, 21, 22, 23, 24, 26, 27, 29 and 32 cm. Distances which cannot be measured out are 12, 17, 20, 25, 28, 30 and 31 cm.

N6   *COLOURING BADGES, MAINLY* (pages 9–12)

1. 6 different badges

2. 12 badges

3. 12 colours of crackers

4. 6 different flags

5. 18 badges

6. 18 badges

7. 24 badges

8. 24 badges

9. 18 badges

N7   *COLOUR SELECTIONS* (pages 13–14)

1. 10 triangles

2. 20 triangles

3. 21 squares

4. 5-bead necklaces: 6; 6-bead necklaces: 11.

5. Twelve ways of colouring 2 red, 1 green and 1 blue section; 12×3, or 36 ways, for all colour choices.

N8   *DOMINOES* (pages 15–17)

2/4 indicates a 2 dot–4 dot domino; 0/0 a double blank.

1. Six ways:
   2/2 and 0/0   3/1 and 0/0   4/0 and 0/0   2/1 and 1/0
   3/0 and 1/0   2/0 and 1/1

2. Ten ways:
   3/2 and 0/0   4/1 and 0/0   5/0 and 0/0   4/0 and 1/0
   3/1 and 1/0   2/2 and 1/0   2/1 and 1/1   2/1 and 2/0
   3/0 and 1/1   3/0 and 2/0

3. Eight ways:
    4/0, 1/0 and 0/0   3/1, 1/0 and 0/0
    2/2, 1/0 and 0/0   3/0, 2/0 and 0/0
    3/0, 1/1 and 0/0   2/1, 2/0 and 0/0
    2/1, 1/1 and 0/0   2/0, 1/1 and 1/0

4. Ten ways:
    5/1 + 0/1   5/0 + 0/2   4/6 + 0/6   4/0 + 1/2
    4/1 + 1/1   4/2 + 1/0   3/6 + 1/6   3/0 + 2/2
    3/1 + 2/1   3/2 + 2/0

5. Fourteen ways:
    6/2 − 2/0   6/3 − 2/1   6/4 − 2/2   6/5 − 2/3
    6/6 − 2/4   5/2 − 1/0   5/3 − 1/1   5/4 − 1/2
    5/5 − 1/3   5/6 − 1/4   4/3 − 0/1   4/4 − 0/2
    4/5 − 0/3   4/6 − 0/4

N9   UNEQUAL PARTITIONING OF SETS (pages 18–19)

1. 36 red and 29 white beads

2. 23 red, 19 white and 16 yellow beads

3. 13 red, 12 white, 6 green and 5 blue buttons

4. 17 green, 12 red, 9 blue and 2 white cubes

N10   HOW MANY AND HOW OLD? (pages 20–1)

1. 18, 15, 12 and 9 years of age

2. 18 sweets

3. 7 sweets

4. Jane has 22 coins, Kylie has 18 coins and Zamund has 10 coins. Altogether they have 50 coins.

N11   INSERTING MISSING NUMBERS IN DIAGRAMS TO FULFIL PARTICULAR REQUIREMENTS (pages 22–6)

1. Rows, columns and diagonals add to 9:

2	4	3	or	3	4	2
4	3	2		2	3	4
3	2	4		4	2	3

2. Three solutions:

> 1 in middle, with $(6,1,3)$, $(2,1,7)$ and $(5,1,4)$ in the rows
> 4 in middle, with $(6,4,2)$, $(5,4,3)$ and $(7,4,1)$ in the rows
> 7 in middle, with $(6,7,1)$, $(3,7,4)$ and $(5,7,2)$ in the rows

3. Three solutions:

> 1 in middle and $(6,1,5)$, $(9,1,2)$, $(8,1,3)$ and $(7,1,4)$ in the rows
> 5 in middle and $(6,5,4)$, $(7,5,3)$, $(8,5,2)$ and $(9,5,1)$ in the rows
> 9 in middle and $(5,9,4)$, $(6,9,3)$, $(7,9,2)$ and $(8,9,1)$ in the rows

4. One solution:

> 1 in the middle and $(7,1,5)$, $(9,1,3)$ and $(10,1,2)$ in the rows

5. Two ways:

> 3 in the middle with rows or columns containing $(9,3,5)$ and $(8,3,6)$
> 9 in the middle with rows or columns containing $(6,9,5)$ and $(8,9,3)$

6. Fourteen possible solutions:

Number in middle	Numbers in rows or columns	Totals
1	$(6,1,3)$ and $(5,1,4)$	10
1	$(5,1,3)$ and $(6,1,2)$	9
1	$(3,1,4)$ and $(2,1,5)$	8
2	$(6,2,1)$ and $(4,2,3)$	9
2	$(6,2,3)$ and $(5,2,4)$	11
3	$(1,3,5)$ and $(2,3,4)$	9
3	$(5,3,2)$ and $(6,3,1)$	10
4	$(6,4,2)$ and $(5,4,3)$	12
4	$(6,4,1)$ and $(5,4,2)$	11
5	$(6,5,1)$ and $(4,5,3)$	12
5	$(4,5,1)$ and $(3,5,2)$	10
6	$(4,6,3)$ and $(5,6,2)$	13
6	$(5,6,1)$ and $(4,6,2)$	12
6	$(4,6,1)$ and $(3,6,2)$	11

7. Seven different solutions:

> 6 in the centre with outer numbers 0, 1, 2 and 3
> 7 in the centre with outer numbers 0, 1, 2 and 4
> 8 in the centre with outer numbers 0, 1, 2 and 5
> 8 in the centre with outer numbers 0, 1, 3 and 4
> 9 in the centre with outer numbers 0, 1, 2 and 6
> 9 in the centre with outer numbers 0, 1, 3 and 5
> 9 in the centre with outer numbers 0, 2, 3 and 4

8. Five different solutions:

> 5 in the centre with outer numbers $1, 2, 3$ and 4
> 6 in the centre with outer numbers $1, 2, 4$ and 5
> 7 in the centre with outer numbers $1, 3, 4$ and 6
> 7 in the centre with outer numbers $2, 3, 4$ and 5
> 7 in the centre with outer numbers $1, 2, 5$ and 6

9. Four different solutions:

> 4 in the centre with outer numbers $1, 2, 3$ and 6
> 5 in the centre with outer numbers $1, 3, 4$ and 7
> 5 in the centre with outer numbers $2, 3, 4$ and 6
> 6 in the centre with outer numbers $2, 4, 5$ and 7

10. Two solutions:

> $(1, 5, 9, 2)$, $(2, 4, 8, 3)$ and $(1, 6, 7, 3)$ on each side
> $(1, 6, 8, 2)$, $(2, 5, 7, 3)$ and $(1, 4, 9, 3)$ on each side

11. Two solutions:

> $(7, 6, 2, 8)$, $(8, 1, 5, 9)$ and $(7, 3, 4, 9)$ on each side
> $(7, 5, 3, 8)$, $(8, 2, 4, 9)$ and $(7, 1, 6, 9)$ on each side

12. Two solutions:

> $(5, 6, 4, 8)$, $(8, 2, 3, 10)$ and $(5, 7, 1, 10)$ on each side
> $(5, 7, 3, 8)$, $(8, 4, 1, 10)$ and $(5, 6, 2, 10)$ on each side

13. Four solutions:

> $(1, 6, 3)$, $(3, 2, 5)$ and $(1, 4, 5)$ on each side
> $(4, 1, 6)$, $(6, 3, 2)$ and $(2, 5, 4)$ on each side
> $(1, 5, 3)$, $(3, 4, 2)$ and $(1, 6, 2)$ on each side
> $(5, 3, 4)$, $(4, 2, 6)$ and $(5, 1, 6)$ on each side

14. Greatest difference: 22, obtained with 6 in the centre and $1, 3, 2, 4$, in that order, in the corners.

15. Greatest difference: 23, obtained with $5, 3$ (or $5, 2$) in the top row, $1, 6$ in the middle row and $4, 2$ (or $4, 3$) in the bottom row.
   Least difference: 11, obtained with $6, 5$ in the top row, $4, 3$ in the middle row and $2, 1$ in the bottom row.

N12 HOW MANY? NUMBERS OF THINGS FROM TWO OR THREE CATEGORIES (pages 27–30)

1. 7 guinea-pigs

2. 4 rabbits and 13 chickens

3.   12 dogs and 10 people, so there were more dogs than people

4.   10 pigeons and 15 rabbits

5.   2 tricycles and 5 bicycles *or* 4 tricycles and 2 bicycles

6.   7 stools and 2 chairs *or* 3 stools and 5 chairs

7.   Spiders have 8 legs and beetles have 6 legs: 5 beetles and 3 spiders *or* 1 beetle and 6 spiders

8.   8 six-wheelers and 2 four-wheelers *or*
        6 six-wheelers and 5 four-wheelers *or*
        4 six-wheelers and 8 four-wheelers *or*
        2 six-wheelers and 11 four-wheelers

9.   5 Chokkies and 14 Fruities *or*
        10 Chokkies and 10 Fruities *or*
        15 Chokkies and 6 Fruities *or*
        20 Chokkies and 2 Fruities

10. Rachel bought 4 chocolate and 9 fruit sweets; Dennis bought 8 chocolate and 6 fruit sweets; John bought 12 chocolate and 3 fruit sweets.

11. 1 triangle, 1 rectangle and 1 pentagon *or*
        3 rectangles *or* 2 triangles and 1 hexagon

12. 1 Mintie, 4 Toffos and 1 Fruito *or*
        6 Minties, 1 Toffo and 1 Fruito *or*
        2 Minties, 2 Toffos and 2 Fruitos
        6 Minties, 1 Toffo and 1 Fruito would provide the most packets: 8

13. 5 Fizzos, 1 Fruitie and 1 Chewie *or*
        3 Fizzos, 2 Fruities and 1 Chewie *or*
        1 Fizzo, 3 Fruities and 1 Chewie *or*
        2 Fizzos, 1 Fruitie and 2 Chewies

14. 1 tricycle, 1 bicycle and 4 unicycles *or*
        1 tricycle, 2 bicycles and 2 unicycles *or*
        2 tricycles, 1 bicycle and 1 unicycle.

Of these, the latter is the only solution with more tricycles than bicycles, so there were 4 Speedies riding 2 tricycles, 1 bicycle and 1 unicycle.

15. 5 sheep, 2 pigs and 1 cow *or*
        2 sheep, 4 pigs and 1 cow *or*
        3 sheep, 2 pigs and 2 cows *or* 1 sheep, 2 pigs and 3 cows

The greatest number of animals to be bought is 8, the least number, 6.

16. They bought 2 teas, 2 Cokes and 4 coffees.

N13   *AREAS OF RECTANGLES* (page 31)

1.   8 cm long and 6 cm wide

2.   The first carpet is 6 m long and 3 m wide with area 18 m². The second carpet is 5 m long and 4 m wide with area 20 m².

N14   *MONEY – WAYS OF PAYING AMOUNTS, MAINLY* (pages 32–3)

1.   Some possible answers are listed below.

    5 coins: one 50p, one 10p, one 5p, one 2p and one 1p
    6 coins: one 50p, three 5p, one 2p and one 1p
    7 coins: three 20p and four 2p
    8 coins: three 20p, three 2p and two 1p
    9 coins: three 20p, two 2p and four 1p
    10 coins: three 20p, one 2p and six 1p
    11 coins: three 20p and eight 1p
    12 coins: two 20p, two 10p and eight 1p
    13 coins: one 20p, four 10p and eight 1p
    14 coins: six 10p and eight 1p
    15 coins: five 10p, two 5p and eight 1p
    16 coins: four 10p, four 5p and eight 1p
    17 coins: three 10p, six 5p and eight 1p
    18 coins: two 10p, eight 5p and eight 1p

2.   Some possible answers are listed below.

    3 coins: one 50p, one 20p and one 2p
    4 coins: one 50p, two 10p and one 2p
    5 coins: one 50p, one 10p, two 5p and one 2p
    6 coins: one 50p, four 5p and one 2p
    7 coins: one 50p, four 5p and two 1p
    8 coins: seven 10p and one 2p
    16 coins: fourteen 5p and two 1p

3.   Two possible answers are given.

    27 coins: 18 fivepences, 8 pennies and 1 twopence
    27 coins: 17 fivepences, 5 twopences and 5 pennies

4.   Imran had 5 coins: one 50p, one 20p, one 5p, one 2p and one 1p.

5.   The least amount for 7 different coins is £1.88. It was not true that the 7 different coins amounted to £1.86.

6.   One 1p, one 2p, one 5p, one 10p, one 20p, one 50p and one £1 amounts to £1.88. To have at least one of each coin, less than £2, the person would have any amount from £1.88 to £1.99, inclusive.

7. Bananas cost 9p each and apples, 7p each.

8. Amounts of 2p, 5p, 7p, 10p, 12p, 15p and 17p could be paid out, using one 2p, one 5p and one 10p. Using one 1p, one 2p and two 5p coins amounts of 1p, 2p, 3p, 5p, 6p, 7p, 8p, 10p, 11p, 12p and 13p could be paid.

9. There are 11 ways of paying out 10p.

10.

Amount	2p	3p	4p	5p	6p	7p	8p	9p	10p
No. of ways	2	2	3	4	5	6	7	8	11

11.

Number of coins	10p	5p	2p	1p
100				100
99			1	98
98			2	96
97			3	94
96		1		95
96			4	92
95		1	1	93
95			5	90
94		1	2	91
94			6	88
93		1	3	89
93			7	86
92		2		90
92		1	4	87
92			8	84
91	1			90
91		2	1	88
90	1		1	88
90		2	2	86
90		1	6	83

There are 20 ways of making £1 with 90, or more, coins.

N15 PUTTING NUMBERS INTO SETS UNDER PRESCRIBED CONDITIONS (pages 34–5)

1. Move the 1 into the set containing 3, 5 and 6. Each set will then total 15.

2. Each set will total 16; two answers:

(9, 7) and (6, 5, 4, 1) *or*
(9, 6, 1) and (7, 5, 4)

3. Each set will total 17; three answers:

    (9,8) and (7,4,3,2,1) *or*
    (9,7,1) and (8,4,3,2) *or*
    (8,7,2) and (9,4,3,1)

4. Each set will total 24; three ways:

    (12,11,1) and (9,7,5,3) *or*
    (12,9,3) and (11,7,5,1) *or*
    (12,7,5) and (11,9,3,1)

5. Each set will total 13; one way: (11,2) and (8,5) and (9,4)

6. Each set will total 15; nine ways:

    (9,6) and (8,7) and (5,4,3,2,1) *or*
    (9,6) and (8,5,2) and (7,4,3,1) *or*
    (9,6) and (8,4,3) and (7,5,2,1) *or*
    (9,6) and (7,5,3) and (8,4,2,1) *or*
    (9,5,1) and (8,7) and (6,4,3,2) *or*
    (9,4,2) and (8,7) and (6,5,3,1) *or*
    (6,5,4) and (8,7) and (9,3,2,1) *or*
    (7,6,2) and (8,4,3) and (9,5,1) *or*
    (8,6,1) and (7,5,3) and (9,4,2)

7. The numbers outside total 30; those inside total 15.

    (a) Two ways:
        (8,7) inside and (9,6,5,4,3,2,1) outside *or*
        (9,6) inside and (8,7,5,4,3,2,1) outside
    (b) Eight ways:
        (9,5,1) inside and (8,7,6,4,3,2) outside *or*
        (9,4,2) inside and (8,7,6,5,3,1) outside *or*
        (8,6,1) inside and (9,7,5,4,3,2) outside *or*
        (8,5,2) inside and (9,7,6,4,3,1) outside *or*
        (8,4,3) inside and (9,7,6,5,2,1) outside *or*
        (7,6,2) inside and (9,8,5,4,3,1) outside *or*
        (7,5,3) inside and (9,8,6,4,2,1) outside *or*
        (6,5,4) inside and (9,8,7,3,2,1) outside
    (c) Six ways:
        (9,3,2,1) inside and (8,7,6,5,4) outside *or*
        (8,4,2,1) inside and (9,7,6,5,3) outside *or*
        (7,5,2,1) inside and (9,8,6,4,3) outside *or*
        (7,4,3,1) inside and (9,8,6,5,2) outside *or*
        (6,5,3,1) inside and (9,8,7,4,2) outside *or*
        (6,4,3,2) inside and (9,8,7,5,1) outside

8. The sets may contain $(25, 21, 3)$ and $(18, 15, 13, 5)$ *or* $(21, 15, 13)$ and $(25, 18, 5, 3)$ *or* $(18, 15, 13, 3)$ and $(25, 21, 5)$, the difference between their sums being 2.

9. The sets may contain $(48, 27, 15, 9)$ and $(41, 33, 22, 5)$ *or* $(48, 22, 15, 9, 5)$ and $(41, 33, 27)$ *or* $(41, 27, 22, 9)$ and $(48, 33, 15, 5)$, the difference between their sums being 2.

N16   *LETTERS IN WORDS* (page 36)

1. Cow: 41; cat: 24; dog: 26; pig: 32; lion: 50; deer: 32; bear: 26. Lion has the greatest value (50); cat has the least value (24); dog and bear have the same value (26).

Some other animal values:

> hippopotamus (169)   rhinoceros (124)   wildebeest (104)
> mongoose (103)   chimpanzee (100)   guinea-pig (89)
> kangaroo (82)   elephant (81)

2. Some suggestions are:

> Christopher (147)   Adam (19)   Kathryn (97)   Ada (6)

3. Some possibilities are:

> yellow bunting (179)   grey wagtail (128)   long-tailed tit (148)
> green finch (89)   chaffinch (58)   coot (53)
> owl (50)   jay (36)

> chrysanthemum (168)   nasturtium (156)   sunflower (133)
> wallflower (127)   hollyhock (109)   marigold (79)
> peony (75)   lupin (72)   lobelia (56)

> bird's-foot trefoil (193)   scarlet pimpernel (186)   honeysuckle (138)
> wood anemone (124)   lesser celandine (145)   primrose (113)
> foxglove (106)   knapweed (79)   daisy (58)

> horse-chestnut (175)   common oak (100)   sycamore (99)
> crab-apple (74)   hazel (52)   larch (42)
> birch (40)   lime (39)   ash (28)
> beech (23)

> Mississippi (157)   Yangtze (98)   Amazon (70)
> Rhine (54)   Congo (54)   Ganges (53)
> Danube (47)   Nile (40)

> Kyrgyzstan (166)   Czechoslovakia (150)   Yugoslavia (132)
> Venezuela (111)   New Zealand (106)
> Norway (96)   Italy (67)   Peru (60)
> Greece (43)   Cuba (27)

4.   Some possibilities are:

> Christopher (11); Ben, Tom or Joe (3)
> Catherine and Elizabeth (9); Eve, Ann, Zoe (3)
> horse-chestnut (13); oak, ash (3)
> chrysanthemum (13); rose (4)
> Guadalquivir (12); Mississippi (11); Po (2)
> Czechoslovakia (14); Peru, Cuba (4)

N17   *REPEATED USE OF A DIGIT TO MAKE PRESCRIBED NUMBERS*
(pages 37–8)

1. $1 - 1 + 1 - 1 = 0$ $11 - 1 - 1 = 9$
     $(1 + 1) \div (1 + 1) = 1$ $(11 - 1) \times 1 = 10$
     $1 + 1 + 1 - 1 = 2$ $11 + 1 - 1 = 11$
     $(1 + 1 + 1) \times 1 = 3$ $(11 + 1) \times 1 = 12$
     $1 + 1 + 1 + 1 = 4$ $11 + 1 + 1 = 13$

2. $9 + 9 - 9 + (9 \div 9) = 10$ $(99 \div 99) + 9 = 10$
     $9 + (9 \times 9) \div (9 \times 9) = 10$ $(9 + 9) \div (9 + 9) + 9 = 10$

3. $(5 \times 5) + 5 - 5 = 25$ $(5 \times 5 \times 5) \div 5 = 25$ $(5 \times 5) \div (5 \div 5) = 25$

4. $3 + 3 - 3 - 3 = 0$ $(3 \div 3) + 3 - 3 = 1$
     $(3 \div 3) + (3 \div 3) = 2$ $(3 + 3 + 3) \div 3 = 3$
     $[(3 \times 3) + 3] \div 3 = 4$ $3 + (3 + 3) \div 3 = 5$
     $3 + 3 - 3 + 3 = 6$ $3 + 3 + (3 \div 3) = 7$
     $(33 \div 3) - 3 = 8$ $(3 \times 3) + 3 - 3 = 9$
     $(3 \times 3) + (3 \div 3) = 10$

5. $7 + 7 - 7 - 7 = 0$ $(7 \div 7) + 7 - 7 = 1$
     $(7 \div 7) + (7 \div 7) = 2$ $(7 + 7 + 7) \div 7 = 3$
     $(77 \div 7) - 7 = 4$ $7 - (7 + 7) \div 7 = 5$
     $7 + (7 - 7) \times 7 = 7$ $7 + (7 + 7) \div 7 = 9$
     $(77 - 7) \div 7 = 10$ $(77 + 7) \div 7 = 12$
     $7 + 7 - (7 \div 7) = 13$ $7 + 7 + 7 - 7 = 14$
     $7 + 7 + (7 \div 7) = 15$

Six, eight and eleven cannot be written using four 7s.

6. $2 + 2 - 2 - 2 = 0$ $(2 \div 2) \times (2 \div 2) = 1$
     $(2 \div 2) + (2 \div 2) = 2$ $(2 + 2 + 2) \div 2 = 3$
     $2 + 2 + 2 - 2 = 4$ $2 + 2 + (2 \div 2) = 5$
     $(2 \times 2 \times 2) - 2 = 6$ $(2 \times 2) + 2 + 2 = 8$
     $(22 \div 2) - 2 = 9$ $(2 \times 2 \times 2) + 2 = 10$

Seven cannot be written using four 2s.

7. (a) $100 = (9 \times 9) + 9 + 9 + (9 \div 9)$
   (b) $20 = (88 \div 8) + 8 + (8 \div 8)$
   (c) $140 = 77 + 7 + 7 + (7 \times 7)$
   (d) $120 = 66 + 66 - 6 - 6$
   (e) $160 = [(44 - 4) \times 4] + 4 - 4$

N18 FIND THE NUMBER – DIGIT SUMS, DIVISIBILITY AND REMAINDERS (pages 39–40)

1. 44 and 80   4. 161

2. 43 and 61   5. 228

3. 43   6. 49

7. The least number is 26. Other numbers of straws for this to happen are 38, 50, 62, 74, 86 and 98.

8. 59 soldiers

9. 103

N19 MAKING NUMBERS, USING GIVEN DIGITS, TO SATISFY PRESCRIBED CONDITIONS (pages 41–2)

1. 753 752 735 732 725 723 573 572 537 532 527 523
   375 372 357 352 327 325 275 273 257 253 237 235

2. 146 147 164 167 174 176 416 417 461 467 471 476
   614 617 641 647 671 674 714 716 741 746 761 764

3. 652 624 564 524 456 452 264 256

4. 873 843 837 834 783 738 483 438 387 384 378 348

5. Twelve numbers:
   431 421 413 412 341 314 241 214 143 142 134 124

6. 543 534 532 523 453 435 354 352 345 325 253 235

7. 652 625 562 542 526 524 452 425 265 256 254 245

8. 345 354 435 453 534 543

9. Twelve numbers:
   541   514   451   421   415   412   241   214   154   145   142   124

10. Eighteen numbers:
    654   653   645   635   632   623   564   563   546   536   465   456
    365   362   356   326   263   236

N20 OBTAINING AND MAKING NUMBERS USING ADDITION, SUBTRACTION AND MULTIPLICATION (pages 43–4)

Questions 1–6 ask the children to make up their own number statements. These individual responses will need checking.

7. Four different numbers can be made: 80, 62, 44 and 35, so the greatest number is 80, and the least is 35.

8. $23 \times 7 = 161$; $32 \times 7 = 224$; $27 \times 3 = 81$; $72 \times 3 = 216$; $37 \times 2 = 74$; $73 \times 2 = 146$. The numbers 74, 81, 146, 161, 216 and 224 can be made, so the least is 74, and the greatest is 224.

9. The greatest number: $215 = 43 \times 5$.
   The least number: $68 = 34 \times 2$.

10. The greatest number: $653 = 652 + 1$.
    The least number: $41 = 15 + 26 = 16 + 25$.

11. The greatest number: $541 = 542 - 1$.
    The least number: $9 = 24 - 15 = 51 - 42$.

12. The greatest sum: $573 = 542 + 31 = 541 + 32 = 532 + 41 = 531 + 42$.
    The least sum: $159 = 124 + 35 = 125 + 34 = 135 + 24 = 134 + 25$.

13. The greatest difference: $631 = 654 - 23$.
    The least difference: $169 = 234 - 65$.

N21 FINDING MISSING DIGITS INCLUDED IN ADDITION, SUBTRACTION, MULTIPLICATION AND DIVISION (page 45)

1. (a) 64 +   (b) 63 +   (c) 96 +   (d) 127 +   (e) 347 +
        28   29   48   356   287
        ──   ──   ───   ───   ───
        92   92   144   483   634

2. (a) 57 −   (b) 75 −   (c) 69 −   (d) 824 −   (e) 724 −
        29   28   26   167   278
        ──   ──   ──   ───   ───
        28   47   43   657   446

3. (a) $\begin{array}{r} 34 \times \\ 7 \\ \hline 238 \end{array}$ (b) $\begin{array}{r} 46 \times \\ 6 \\ \hline 276 \end{array}$ (c) $\begin{array}{r} 43 \times \\ 7 \\ \hline 301 \end{array}$ (d) $\begin{array}{r} 133 \times \\ 4 \\ \hline 532 \end{array}$ (e) $\begin{array}{r} 156 \times \\ 3 \\ \hline 468 \end{array}$

4. (a) $\begin{array}{r} 228 \\ 4\overline{)912} \end{array}$ (b) $\begin{array}{r} 274 \\ 3\overline{)822} \end{array}$ (c) $\begin{array}{r} 132 \\ 4\overline{)528} \end{array}$ (d) $\begin{array}{r} 149 \\ 5\overline{)745} \end{array}$ (e) $\begin{array}{r} 156 \\ 3\overline{)468} \end{array}$

N22   *NUMBER RELATIONSHIPS INCLUDING MISSING NUMBERS* (page 46)

1. 7   4. 20

2. 18   5. 9 and 365

3. 12   6. 84

N23   *ADDITION WITH LETTERS REPLACING DIGITS* (pages 47–9)

1. $13 + 13 + 13 = 39$ so A = 1, B = 3 and C = 9, *or*
    $14 + 14 + 14 = 42$ so A = 1, B = 4 and C = 2, *or*
    $28 + 28 + 28 = 84$ so A = 2, B = 8 and C = 4

2. $31 + 31 + 31 = 93$ so A = 3, B = 1 and C = 9, *or*
    $24 + 24 + 24 = 72$ so A = 2, B = 4 and C = 7, *or*
    $17 + 17 + 17 = 51$ so A = 1, B = 7 and C = 5

3. $23 + 23 + 23 + 23 = 92$ so A = 2, B = 3 and C = 9

4. $82 + 82 + 82 + 82 = 328$ so A = 8, B = 2 and C = 3

5. $74 + 74 + 74 = 222$ so that A = 7, B = 4 and C = 2, *or*
    $37 + 37 + 37 = 111$ so that A = 3, B = 7 and C = 1

6. $185 + 185 + 185 = 555$ so that A = 1, B = 8 and C = 5

7. $412 + 412 = 824$ so A = 4, B = 1, C = 2 and D = 8, *or*
    $462 + 462 = 924$ so A = 4, B = 6, C = 2 and D = 9, *or*
    $437 + 437 = 874$ so A = 4, B = 3, C = 7 and D = 8, *or*
    $487 + 487 = 974$ so A = 4, B = 8, C = 7 and D = 9

8. There are twelve solutions:

    $\begin{array}{r} 123 + \\ 321 \\ \hline 444 \end{array}$ $\begin{array}{r} 321 + \\ 123 \\ \hline 444 \end{array}$ $\begin{array}{r} 135 + \\ 531 \\ \hline 666 \end{array}$ $\begin{array}{r} 531 + \\ 135 \\ \hline 666 \end{array}$ $\begin{array}{r} 234 + \\ 432 \\ \hline 666 \end{array}$ $\begin{array}{r} 432 + \\ 234 \\ \hline 666 \end{array}$

$$147 + \atop \underline{741} \atop 888 \qquad 741 + \atop \underline{147} \atop 888 \qquad 246 + \atop \underline{642} \atop 888 \qquad 642 + \atop \underline{246} \atop 888 \qquad 345 + \atop \underline{543} \atop 888 \qquad 543 + \atop \underline{345} \atop 888$$

9. There are thirteen solutions:

$$231 + \atop \underline{231} \atop 462 \qquad 271 + \atop \underline{271} \atop 542 \qquad 281 + \atop \underline{281} \atop 562 \qquad 291 + \atop \underline{291} \atop 582 \qquad 432 + \atop \underline{432} \atop 864 \qquad 482 + \atop \underline{482} \atop 964$$

$$216 + \atop \underline{216} \atop 432 \qquad 236 + \atop \underline{236} \atop 472 \qquad 286 + \atop \underline{286} \atop 572 \qquad 417 + \atop \underline{417} \atop 834 \qquad 427 + \atop \underline{427} \atop 854 \qquad 457 + \atop \underline{457} \atop 914 \qquad 467 + \atop \underline{467} \atop 934$$

10. Some possible solutions are:

$$245 + \atop \underline{718} \atop 963 \qquad 219 + \atop \underline{654} \atop 873 \qquad 527 + \atop \underline{364} \atop 891 \qquad 569 + \atop \underline{214} \atop 783 \qquad 618 + \atop \underline{327} \atop 945$$

$$782 + \atop \underline{154} \atop 936 \qquad 681 + \atop \underline{273} \atop 954 \qquad 591 + \atop \underline{273} \atop 864 \qquad 576 + \atop \underline{342} \atop 918 \qquad 692 + \atop \underline{145} \atop 837$$

There are many other solutions.

N24   *ALL DIGITS ONE OUT* (pages 50–1)

1. $28 + \atop \underline{43} \atop 71$ 2. $81 + \atop \underline{16} \atop 97$ 3. $83 - \atop \underline{21} \atop 62$ 4. $54 - \atop \underline{23} \atop 31$

5. $92 - \atop \underline{11} \atop 81$ 6. $37 \times \atop \underline{5} \atop 185$ 7. $37 \times \atop \underline{4} \atop 148$ 8. $47 \times \atop \underline{3} \atop 141$

9. $54 \times \atop \underline{3} \atop 162$ 10. $63 \times \atop \underline{4} \atop 252$

11. $3\overline{)732} \atop 244$ 12. $5\overline{)625} \atop 125$

N25   *INVOLVING PRIME NUMBERS* (pages 52–3)

1. One has only one factor.
    Prime numbers have only two factors: 2, 3, 5, 7, 11, 13, 17, 19, 23 and 29.
    Square numbers 1, 4, 9, 16 and 25 have an odd number of factors.

12, 18, 20 and 28 have six factors, and 24 and 30 have eight factors. 4, 9 and 25 have three factors, 6, 8, 10, 14, 15, 21, 22, 26 and 27 have four factors and 16 has five factors.

2. Prime numbers less than 100:

$$2 \quad 3 \quad 5 \quad 7 \quad 11 \quad 13 \quad 17 \quad 19 \quad 23 \quad 29 \quad 31 \quad 37 \quad 41$$
$$43 \quad 47 \quad 53 \quad 59 \quad 61 \quad 67 \quad 71 \quad 73 \quad 79 \quad 83 \quad 89 \quad 97$$

3. (a) Primes one more than a perfect square: 5, 17 and 37
   (b) Prime, one less than a perfect square: 3
   (c) Prime number, one less than a perfect cube: 7

4. The houses are numbered 49, 51, 53, 55, 57.

5. Numbers which cannot be written as the sum of two primes are 6, 11, 17, 23, 27, 29, 35, 37, 41 and 47; the remaining numbers from 5 to 50, inclusive, can be expressed as the sums of two primes.

6. Check individual attempts. Some possibilities are

$$23 + 41 + 17 + 5 = 86 \qquad 2 + 13 + 71 = 86 \qquad 13 + 73 = 86$$
$$3 + 13 + 19 + 29 = 64 \qquad 2 + 3 + 59 = 64 \qquad 3 + 61 = 64$$
$$29 + 31 + 37 + 19 = 116 \qquad 2 + 17 + 97 = 116 \qquad 43 + 73 = 116$$
$$41 + 43 + 47 + 37 = 168 \qquad 2 + 59 + 107 = 168 \qquad 71 + 97 = 168$$

7. Four prime numbers: 2, 41, 53, 67, *or* 2, 47, 53, 61, *or* 5, 23, 47, 61, *or* 5, 23, 41, 67.

N26 *CONTINUING SEQUENCES* (pages 54–5)

1. 26, 29, 32	8. 38, 47, 57
2. 50, 57, 64	9. 50, 65, 82
3. 79, 90, 101	10. 66, 83, 102
4. 64, 128, 256	11. 137, 172, 211
5. 34, 55, 89	12. 169, 217, 271
6. 64, 81, 100	13. 197, 249, 307
7. 36, 45, 55	14. 191, 383, 767

N27 *PATTERN AND PREDICTION* (pages 56–61)

1. 2, 3, 4, 5, 6, ... ways; 21 ways in the 20th shape.

2. 4, 7, 10, 13, ... matchsticks; 46 matchsticks in the 15th shape.

3. 4, 8, 12, 16, 20, ... matchsticks; 48 matchsticks in the 12th shape.

4. 4, 10, 16, 22, . . .matchsticks; 58 matchsticks in the 10th shape.

5. 4, 12, 20, 28, . . . matchsticks; 100 matchsticks in the 13th shape.

6. 2, 5, 8, 11, 14, . . . squares; 50 squares in the 17th shape.

7. 4, 9, 16, 25, . . . triangles; 81 small triangles in the 8th shape.

8. 4, 10, 18, 28, 40, . . .matchsticks; 88 matchsticks in the 8th shape.

9. 1, 5, 13, 25, 41, . . .squares; 145 small squares in the 9th shape.

10. 4, 13, 26, 43, . . . matchsticks; 151 matchsticks in the 8th shape.

11. 1, 3, 6, 10, 15, . . . rectangles; 55 rectangles in the 10th shape.

12. 1, 3, 6, 10, 15, . . . lines; 66 lines needed to join 12 points.

13. 1, 3, 6, 10, 15, . . . handshakes; 91 handshakes with 14 people.

14. 3, 6, 10, 15, 21, . . . ways; 66 ways in the 10th diagram.

15. 2, 5, 9, 14, 20, . . . diagonals; 35 diagonals in a 10-sided polygon. A polygon could not have 55 diagonals. A 12-sided polygon has 54 diagonals.

16.

Number	1	2	3	4	5	6	7	8	9	10
Number of ways	1	2	3	5	8	13	21	34	55	89

17.

Number of lines	1	2	3	4	5	6	7	8	9	10
Number of parts	2	4	7	11	16	22	29	37	46	56

A circle may be divided into 56 parts with 10 straight lines.

18. 3, 9, 18, 30, 45, . . . rectangles; 108 rectangles in the 8th shape.

19. 1, 5, 14, 30, 55, 91, . . . squares; 204 squares in the 8th shape.

N28 *VARIOUS GAMES* (pages 62–4)

1.

Triangle number	1st	2nd	3rd	4th	5th	6th	7th
Number of moves	1	2	3	5	7	9	12

2. Thirteen moves.

3. $1, 3, 6, 10, 15, 21, \ldots$ moves; 55 moves to rearrange 10 black and 10 white counters.

4. $3, 8, 15, 24, 35, 48, \ldots$ moves; 80 moves to rearrange the 8 black and 8 white counters.

5. $3, 5, 7, 9, 11, \ldots$ moves; 41 moves to exchange the rows of counters.

6. $3, 7, 15, 31, 63, \ldots$ moves for $2, 3, 4, 5, 6, \ldots$ rings; a minimum number of 127 moves required to rebuild a 7-ring tower.

N29 *A THOUSANDS MIXTURE* (pages 65–6)

1. 8631 8613 8361 8316 8163 8136 6831 6813
    6381 6318 6183 6138 3861 3816 3681 3618
    3186 3168 1863 1836 1683 1638 1386 1368

2. 9654 9645 9564 9546 9465 9456 6954 6945
    6594 6549 6495 6459 5964 5946 5694 5649
    5496 5469 4965 4956 4695 4659 4596 4569

3. The greatest sum: $1025 = 973 + 52 = 972 + 53 = 952 + 73$.
The least sum: $296 = 237 + 59 = 239 + 57 = 259 + 37$.

4. The greatest sum: $1573 = 842 + 731 = 832 + 741 = 831 + 742$.
The least sum: $385 = 137 + 248 = 148 + 237 = 138 + 247$.

5.
$$
\begin{array}{cccc}
3524\ + & 48\ + & 243\ \times & 356\ \times \\
\underline{5657} & \underline{973} & \underline{7} & \underline{4} \\
9181 & 1021 & 1701 & 1424
\end{array}
$$

6.
$$
\begin{array}{cc}
243\ \times & 634\ \times \\
\underline{5} & \underline{4} \\
1215 & 2536
\end{array}
$$

N30 *FINDING, WITH A CALCULATOR, THOSE NUMBERS WHICH DIVIDE EXACTLY BY THEIR DIGIT SUMS* (pages 67–8)

1. The twelve numbers are $195, 285, 375, 555, 645, 690, 735, 780, 825, 870, 915$ and 960.

2. The eight numbers are $192, 228, 264, 336, 372, 408, 444$ and 480.

3. The twelve numbers are $114, 132, 150, 204, 222, 240, 312, 330, 402, 420, 510$ and 600.

4. $476, 629, 782$ and 935.

5. $247, 364, 481, 715$ and 832.

6. Only 874.

7. Other numbers are $1679, 3749, 3956, 4577, 4784$ and 4991.

N31 *MULTIPLICATION INVOLVING THE USE OF A CALCULATOR* (pages 69–70)

1. The greatest number: $1312 = 32 \times 41$

2. The greatest number: $1632 = 51 \times 32$
    The least number: $235 = 235 \times 1$

3. The rectangle is $86\,cm$ long and $43\,cm$ wide.

4. The rectangle is $165\,cm$ long and $55\,cm$ wide.

5. The two consecutive numbers: $56, 57$. $56 \times 57 = 3192$
    The three consecutive numbers: $26, 27, 28$. $26 \times 27 \times 28 = 19656$

6. The greatest product: $34074 = 631 \times 54$
    The least product: $4984 = 356 \times 14$

7. The greatest product: $136396 = 61 \times 52 \times 43$
    The least product: $12600 = 14 \times 25 \times 36$

8. The greatest product: $342002 = 631 \times 542$
    The least product: $33210 = 135 \times 246$

9. The greatest product: $484526 = 742 \times 653$
    The least product: $87822 = 246 \times 357$

10. 36 and 1369 *or* 676 and 729: $36 + 1369 = 676 + 729 = 1405$

11. 25 large tins and 31 small tins.

N32 *INVOLVING PALINDROMES* (page 71)

1. There are 90 three-digit palindromes:

999, 989, 979, . . . , 919, 909   898, 888, 878, . . . , 818, 808
797, 787, 777, . . . , 717, 707   696, 686, 676, . . . , 616, 606
595, 585, 575, . . . , 515, 505   494, 484, 474, . . . , 414, 404
393, 383, 373, . . . , 313, 303   292, 282, 272, . . . , 212, 202
191, 181, 171, . . . , 111, 101

There are 90 four-digit palindromes:

9999, 9889, 9779, . . . , 9119, 9009   8998, 8888, 8778, . . . , 8118, 8008
7997, 7887, 7777, . . . , 7117, 7007   6996, 6886, 6776, . . . , 6116, 6006
5995, 5885, 5775, . . . , 5115, 5005   4994, 4884, 4774, . . . , 4114, 4004
3993, 3883, 3773, . . . , 3113, 3003   2992, 2882, 2772, . . . , 2112, 2002
1991, 1881, 1771, . . . , 1111, 1001

2. 1983 has no palindromic dates because no month has 38 days.
Ten palindromic dates for 1991: 19–1–91, 19–2–91, 19–3–91,
19–4–91, 19–5–91, 19–6–91, 19–7–91, 19–8–91, 19–9–91, 19–11–91.
Ten palindromic dates for 1992: 29–1–92, 29–2–92, 29–3–92,
29–4–92, 29–5–92, 29–6–92, 29–7–92, 29–8–92, 29–9–92, 29–11–92.
After 1991, there are only 10 more palindromic dates before 2001.

3. 29 and 1725 require 1 step; 85, 67, 371, 329 and 179 require 2 steps; 796 and 376 need 3 steps; 678 needs 4 steps; 9876 needs 5 steps; and 197 and 287 need 7 steps.

N33 *FINDING NUMBERS WITH PARTICULAR PROPERTIES* (pages 72–3)

1. All numbers from 3 to 50, inclusive, can be expressed as the sum of two or more consecutive numbers except 4, 8, 16 and 32.

2. Numbers, less than 50, with an odd number of factors are 1, 4, 9, 16, 25, 36 and 49. This allows the prediction that 64 and 81 will also have an odd number of factors. Check this. 64 has 7 factors: 1, 2, 4, 8, 16, 32 and 64. 81 has 5 factors: 1, 3, 9, 27 and 81.

3. There are 40 such numbers:

994	984	974	964	954	944	934	924	914	904
893	883	873	863	853	843	833	823	813	803
792	782	772	762	752	742	732	722	712	702
691	681	671	661	651	641	631	621	611	601

4.   There are 80 such numbers:

998	988	978	968	958	948	938	928	918	908
897	887	877	867	857	847	837	827	817	807
796	786	776	766	756	746	736	726	716	706
695	685	675	665	655	645	635	625	615	605
594	584	574	564	554	544	534	524	514	504
493	483	473	463	453	443	433	423	413	403
392	382	372	362	352	342	332	322	312	302
291	281	271	261	251	241	231	221	211	201

5.   There are 30 such numbers:

492	491	482	481	472	471	462	461	452	451
442	441	432	431	422	421	412	411	402	401
391	381	371	361	351	341	331	321	311	301

Answers to Shape and Space Activities

S1 MATCHSTICK PUZZLES (pages 77–8)

1.

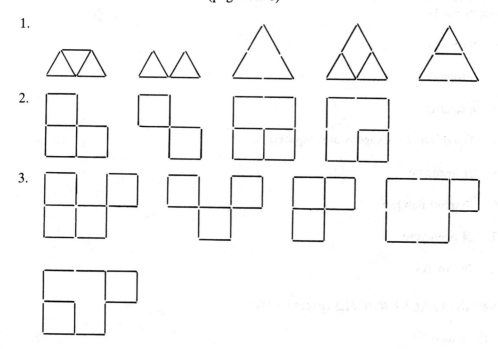

2.

3.

S2 FINDING GIVEN SHAPES WITHIN VARIOUS DIAGRAMS (pages 79–82)

1. (a) 5 triangles   (b) 9 triangles   (c) 11 triangles

2. 6 quadrilaterals

3. (a) 10 rectangles   (b) 11 rectangles

4. 10 squares

5. (a) 3 triangles, 5 quadrilaterals and 5 pentagons
   (b) 4 triangles, 2 quadrilaterals and 5 pentagons

6. (a) 13 triangles   (b) 16 triangles   (c) 16 triangles

7. 18 squares

8. (a) 20 triangles   (b) 22 triangles

9. (a) 18 rectangles   (b) 25 rectangles

10. 27 triangles

11. 32 squares

S3   *DRAWING GIVEN SHAPES ON SQUARE DOT LATTICE PAPER* (pages 83–4)

1.   8 triangles

2.   8 triangles

3.   6 squares

4.   Ten different hexagons are required.

5.   21 hexagons

6.   16 quadrilaterals

7.   24 pentagons

8.   20 squares

S4   *DIFFERENT ROUTES* (pages 85–90)

1.   6 ways

2.   12 ways

3.   6 ways

4.   (a) 4 ways   (b) 8 ways   (c) 10 ways

5.   10 ways

6.   14 ways

7.   17 ways

8.   12 ways

9.   20 ways

10.   (a) 3 ways   (b) 4 ways   (c) 6 ways   (d) 6 ways   (e) 8 ways

S5   *CONCERNING AREA* (pages 91–3)

1.   6 different ways

2.   20 different ways

3. There are 7 other ways involving non-identical halves.

4. Shapes can be drawn with 12 sides.

6. 8 shapes can be drawn with areas of 3 squares

10. 23 different shapes can be drawn with areas of 2 squares.

11. 22 different ways of halving the square.

12. At least 28 different ways can be found.

14. Squares with areas of 1, 2, 4, 5, 8, 9, 10, 13, 16, 17, 18, 20, 25, 26, 29, 32, 34, 36, 37 and 40 can be drawn.

15. A shape can be drawn with 18 sides.

S6   *ARRANGEMENTS WITH STAMPS* (pages 94–6)

1. 5 ways   6. 20 ways

2. 6 ways   7. 10 ways

3. 6 ways   8. 15 ways

4. 12 ways   9. 20 ways

5. 12 ways   10. 30 ways

S7   *FITTING TOGETHER SQUARES AND OBLONGS, MAINLY* (pages 97–8)

1. Six ways of tearing out 3 attached stamps

2. 19 different arrangements of 4 attached stamps

3. 31 different ways:
    19 ways with 4 attached stamps (see Qu. 2)
    6 ways for 3 attached stamps and one other (see Qu. 1)
    3 ways of receiving two lots of 2 attached stamps
    2 ways of receiving 2 joined stamps and 2 separate stamps
    1 way of receiving 4 separate stamps

4. 5 ways

5. 12 ways

6. 1 way of joining 2 cubes; 2 ways to join 3 cubes; 5 ways of joining 4 cubes; 12 ways of joining 5 cubes

7. Four squares can be joined in 5 ways, five squares can be joined in 12 ways.

S8 *MAKING SHAPES BY FITTING TOGETHER PAPER TRIANGLES AND RECTANGLES* (pages 99–100)

1. Four shapes can be made

2. Seven shapes can be made

3. Ten shapes can be made

S9 *FOLDING PAPER SHAPES* (pages 101–2)

1. A rectangle when folded will produce 4-, 5-, 6-, 7-, 8- and 9-sided shapes.
    An equilateral triangle when folded will produce 3-, 4-, 5-, 6- and 7-sided shapes.
    A square when folded will produce 3-, 4-, 5-, 6- and 9-sided shapes.
    A regular hexagon when folded will produce 4-, 5-, 6-, 7-, 10- and 13-sided shapes.

2. A rectangle can be divided in four ways: (3,3), (3,4), (3,5) and (4,4).

    (a) Triangle: (3,3) and (3,4).
    (b) Regular pentagon: (3,4), (3,5), (3,6), (4,4) and (4,5).
    (c) Regular hexagon: (3,5), (3,6), (3,7), (4,4), (4,5), (4,6) and (5,5).
    (d) Regular octagon: (3,7), (3,8), (3,9), (4,6), (4,7), (4,8), (5,5), (5,6), (5,7) and (6,6).

3. Equilateral triangle: (3,3,3), (3,3,4), (3,4,4), (3,3,4,4), (3,3,3,4) and (3,4,4,4).

    (a) Rectangle:
        (3,3,3), (3,3,4), (3,3,5), (3,3,6), (3,4,5), (4,4,4), (3,3,3,3), (3,3,3,5), (3,3,4,4), (3,3,4,5), (3,3,4,6), (3,3,5,5), (3,4,4,5) and (4,4,4,4).
    (b) Some ways of dividing a regular pentagon:
        (3,3,3), (3,3,4), (3,3,5), (3,4,4), (3,4,6), (3,3,3,4), (3,3,3,5), (3,3,3,6), (3,3,4,4), (3,3,4,5), (3,3,4,6), (3,4,4,4), (4,4,4,4) and (4,4,4,5).
    (c) Some ways of dividing a regular hexagon:
        (3,3,4), (3,4,5), (3,5,6), (4,4,4), (4,4,6), (4,5,5), (3,3,4,4), (4,4,4,4) and (4,4,5,5).
    (d) Some ways of dividing a regular octagon:
        (3,3,6), (3,4,5), (4,4,4), (4,4,6), (4,5,7), (4,4,4,4), (3,3,5,5), (4,4,6,6) and (5,5,5,5).

S10 *DRAWING LINES AND JOINING DOTS* (pages 103–4)

1. 4 dots can be joined with 3, 5 and 6 lines.
   5 dots can be joined with 4, 7, 8, 9 and 10 lines.
   6 dots can be joined with 5, 9, 11, 12, 13, 14 and 15 lines.
   7 dots can be joined with 6, 11, 12, 14, 15, 16, 17, 19, 20 and 21 lines.

2. 3 lines can divide a circle into 4, 5, 6 and 7 parts.
   4 lines can divide a circle into 5, 6, 7, 8, 9, 10 and 11 parts.
   5 lines can divide a circle into 6, 7, 8, 9, . . ., 14, 15 and 16 parts.
   6 lines can divide a circle into 7, 8, 9, . . ., 20, 21 and 22 parts.

3.

Number of dots	2	3	4	5	6	7
Number of parts	2	4	8	16	31	57

The sequence 2, 4, 8, 16, . . . suggests that 6 and 7 dots will divide a circle into 32 and 64 parts. These predictions are incorrect, the true values being 31 and 57.

Answers to Puzzlers

P1   WHERE ARE THEY? (pages 107–8)

1. From left to right – white, black and green counters

2. From left to right – blue, red and orange counters

3. From left to right – blue, red, orange and green stamps

4. From left to right – brown, cream, green and white houses

5. From left to right, facing you – Brian, Yvonne, Gemma and Peter

6. From left to right – 5p, 1p, 20p, 2p and 10p coins

P2   NAME THE ANIMALS (pages 109–10)

1. Princess is the horse.

2. Richard has a mouse, Jean has a guinea-pig and Katherine has a rabbit.

3. Patch is a dog and Ginger is a cat.

4. Gertie is a pig, Duke is a horse and Omar is a camel.

5. Garth is a horse, Patch is a dog and Winnie is a mouse.

6. Robert has a dog, Dora has a cat and Catherine has a rabbit.

7. Rebecca's favourite animal was a sea-lion, David's was a giraffe and Shabinah's was an elephant.

8. Hector is the dog, Susie is the mouse and Jason is a cat.

9. Noble is the horse, Prince is the dog, Tiny is the mouse and Rosie is the cat.

P3   FAMILY MATTERS (page 111)

1. Ruth and William belong to one family, Diane and Paul to the other.

2. Eleanor and Graham are in one family, Nicholas and Karen in the other.

3. Julie and Nathan are both aged 4.

P4   *PUTTING THINGS IN ORDER* (pages 112–13)

1.   Alison is shortest; Duane is tallest.

2.   Susan is 14, Glenn is 12 and Eddie is 9.

3.   Steve is 12, Natalie is 10, Greg is 9 and Sîan is 7.

4.   Janet is 14, Bill is 12, Stella is 10 and Matthew is 8.

5.   Ken scored 24 goals, Robert scored 20, Osman scored 12 and Gary scored only 8.

P5   *WHAT'S WHAT?* (pages 114–16)

1.   Mrs Adams has a red car, Mrs Hill has a green car and Mrs Young has a blue car.

2.   Betty bought chocolate, Lizzie bought lemonade and Fatima bought an ice-cream.

3.   Mrs Green bought apples, Mr Baker bought grapes and Mrs Smith bought bananas.

4.   The white crocuses were in the green bowl, the blue ones were in the white bowl and the yellow crocuses were in the brown bowl.

5.   Mr Ahmed has a grey car, Mr Wilson a blue car and Mrs Hall a brown car.

6.   White is the chef and Grey is the pilot; Black is the sailor.

7.   Edward Davis, James Evans and Diana Jones

8.   Mary Brown, Tracey Cook and June Scott

9.   George Black, Marie Price and Alice Farmer

10. Lizzie Allen, Jill Roberts and Don Clark

11. Sophie Taylor, Derek Russell and Jessica Wood

12. Henry Carter, Gerald Atkins and Keith Watts

13. Ben Adams, Anne Baker, Dennis Cook and Catherine Davis

14. Carol has the shortest pencil which is black. Lucy has the longest pencil which is red. Sharon has a blue pencil.

15. Lucille wears a white blouse and blue skirt. Claire wears a green blouse and brown skirt. Rhiannon wears a pink blouse and grey skirt.

16. Sally has black hair and wears a navy blue skirt. Charlotte has brown hair and wears a green skirt. Lynda has fair hair and wears a grey skirt.

P6 *MEASURING OUT LIQUID* (pages 117–18)

1. Fill the 3-litre measure twice and use the contents to fill the 5-litre measure. This leaves 1 litre in the 3-litre measure.

2. Fill the 3-litre measure three times and use this amount to fill the 8-litre measure. This will leave 1 litre in the 3-litre measure.

3. Filling the 2-litre measure three times, pouring the contents into the 5-litre measure to fill it, leaves 1 litre in the 2-litre measure.
   Filling the 5-litre measure, pouring into the 2-litre measure to fill it, leaves 3 litres in the 5-litre measure.

4. Filling the 3-litre measure twice, pouring the contents into the 4-litre measure to fill it, leaves 2 litres in the 3-litre vessel.
   Filling the 4-litre measure, pouring into the 3-litre vessel to fill it, leaves 1 litre in the 4-litre vessel.

5. Filling the 8-litre measure twice and emptying the contents into the 5-litre measure three times, leaves 1 litre in the 8-litre vessel.
   Amounts of 2, 3, 4, 5, 6 and 7 litres can all be measured out.

P7 *CROSSING THE RIVER* (page 119)

Two boys cross – one boy returns – one man crosses – one boy returns – two boys cross – one boy returns – one man crosses – one boy returns – two boys cross.

P8 *FIND THE HEAVIEST* (page 120)

1. Arrange the marbles in threes.
   Put two lots of three on the balance. If one side goes down this set contains the heavier marble. If they balance, however, the heavier marble is one of the three in the remaining set.
   Put two of the marbles from the heavier set of three on the balance. If one side goes down it holds the heavier marble. If they balance the heavier marble is the remaining one.

2. Divide the coins into three sets of nine coins.
   Compare two sets of nine on the balance to determine which of these sets contains the heavier coin, if either, or whether it is included in the remaining unbalanced set.
   Split the heavier set of nine coins into three sets of three coins.
   Compare two sets of three on the balance to find which of these contains the heavier coin, if either, or whether it is included in the remaining set of three coins.
   Split the heavier set of three into separate coins. Compare two of these on the balance and find which of these, if either, or the remaining one is the heavier coin.

P9   FIND THE NUMBER (pages 121–2)

Six questions are necessary to find a number less than 50; seven questions to find a number less than 100; and eight questions to find a number less than 200.

P10   WHO'S 'IT'? (page 123)

1. The count would start with Christine for Adrian to be 'it'.

2. The sentence would start with Laura for Laura to be 'it'.

3. The sentence would start with Christine for Christine to be 'it'.

4. The sentence would start with Adrian for Phil to be 'it'.

P11   FREE OFFERS (page 124)

1. Nine free jars of coffee could be obtained.

2. The least number of bars of soap to be bought is nine.

3. Eight packets of jelly need to be purchased.

P12   NUMBERS FOR LETTERS (pages 125–6)

1. 10: letters in the word 'chimpanzee'.

2. 18: rose starts with r, the 18th letter of the alphabet.

3. 59: letter total if a = 1, b = 2, c = 3, d = 4, and so on.

4. 9: 3 vowels and 3 consonants, giving $3 \times 3 = 9$.

5. 3: 4 consonants and 1 vowel, giving $4 - 1 = 3$.

6. 8: 3 vowels and 2 consonants, giving $(3 \times 2) + 2 = 8$, using the rule, 'twice the number of vowels, add the number of consonants'.

P13 *MISSING LINKS* (page 127)

1. $6 + 8 - 5 = 9$

2. $(8 - 1) \times 4 = 28$

3. $(10 \div 2) + 3 = 8$

4. $3 * 8 = (3 \times 8) - 4 = 20$

5. $2 * 5 = 2 \times 2 \times 5 = 20$

P14 *INCONSECUTIVE NUMBERS* (pages 128–9)

1.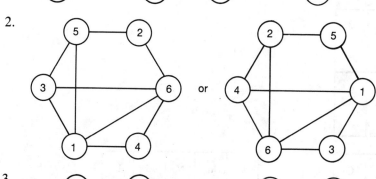

2.

3.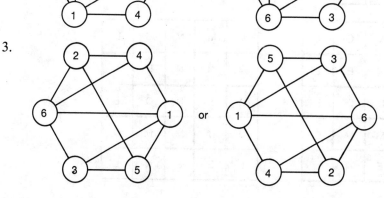

4.

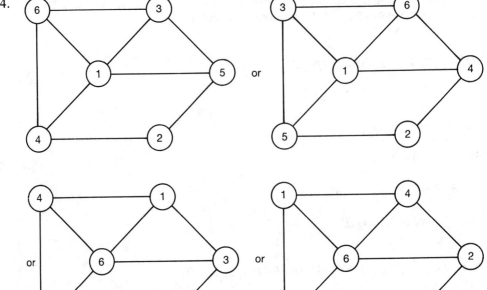

P15   *CUTTING UP SQUARES* (pages 130–1)

1.

A	C	C	B
B	B	D	A
D	A	D	B
D	C	C	A

2.

L	M	M	O	L
O	N	N	E	L
O	E	N	O	E
N	M	M	M	O
L	E	E	N	L

or

L	M	M	O	L
O	N	N	E	L
O	E	N	O	E
N	M	M	M	O
L	E	E	N	L

3.

Q	A	U	U	U	S
Q	R	S	S	A	A
A	E	S	Q	R	R
U	E	R	S	E	Q
U	R	R	U	A	E
E	A	S	Q	Q	E

P16   *MISPRINTS* (pages 132–3)

1. Rows and columns add to 15. The third number to the right, bottom row, should be 2 and not 3.

2. Rows and columns add to 20. The second number to the right, third row, should be 2 and not 3.

3. Rows and columns add to 30. The third number to the right, second row, should be 10 and not 11.

4. Rows and columns add to 50. The third number to the right, third row, should be 17 and not 16.

P17   *NUMBERS FOR SYMBOLS* (pages 134–5)

1. Second row total 14; 4th row total 17; 2nd column total 10.

2. Third row total 9; 4th row total 11; 2nd column total 20.

3. Third row total 13; 4th row total 11; 1st column total 11.

P18   *MAGIC SQUARES* (pages 136–7)

47	58	69	80	1	12	23	34	45
57	68	79	9	11	22	33	44	46
67	78	8	10	21	32	43	54	56
77	7	18	20	31	42	53	55	66
6	17	19	30	41	52	63	65	76
16	27	29	40	51	62	64	75	5
26	28	39	50	61	72	74	4	15
36	38	49	60	71	73	3	14	25
37	48	59	70	81	2	13	24	35